D1580985

DANIEL O'CONNELL

A Graphic Life

DAINGEAN

2 8 SEP 2022

WITHDRAWN

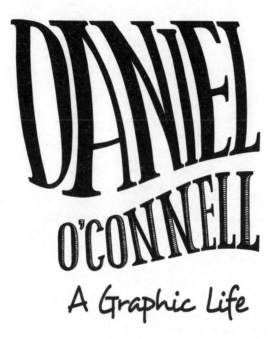

DANIEL O'CONNELL

A Graphic Life

JODY MOYLAN

Illustrated by
Mateusz Nowakowski

The Collins Press

FIRST PUBLISHED IN 2016 BY
The Collins Press
West Link Park
Doughcloyne
Wilton
Cork
T12 N5EF
Ireland

A CIP record for this book is available from the British Library.

Paperback ISBN: 978-1-84889-269-9
PDF eBook ISBN: 978-1-84889-569-0
EPUB eBook ISBN: 978-1-84889-570-6
Kindle ISBN: 978-1-84889-571-3

Design and typesetting by Burns Design
Typeset in Athelas
Printed in Poland by Hussar Books

Cover design by Mateusz Nowakowski

CONTENTS

PROLOGUE

In a Munster village, one summer's evening in the year 1822, a man entered the local inn. He sat down beside the window and looked out upon the street. It was market day but now, as the sun was setting, the place was becoming deserted. The man shuffled and moved from his seat to another, to avoid the glare that was filtering in. He now had a better view of the long, curved street.

He sat and watched as a plume of dust rose up at its end, and out of which came a horse-drawn carriage. As it edged closer the coachman urged his horses on and soon swept around the angle of the street. The man got up from his seat to crane his neck out the window of the inn.

He watched as the carriage rolled up with increased force and thundering sound, before it came to a sudden halt. The door of the carriage was thrown open and the occupant leapt out. The man at the window did not know who it was, but the imposing stranger made an instant impression. With shoulders broad, he stood robust and strong at almost 6 feet tall. He had on his head a light fur cap that was partly thrown back, and displayed a fine forehead, which the local man took to be a sign of great genius. There was a glint in the stranger's light-blue eyes, but his face was pale, and reflected a life of study, work and turmoil. It was as though some greater purpose had stolen from him the glow of health and youth.

1

This mysterious outsider stood silent and gazed at the ground, as if transfixed on some important business to come. His cravat was untied and hung loosely around his neck. One hand sat in his waistcoat pocket, while the other hung free by his side. The man at the window thought the stranger would make a great figure for a painter of fine art.

'Quick with the horses,' the stranger shouted. Once they were changed, and new ones fastened, the stranger hurriedly re-entered his carriage. As quickly as he had arrived, he was gone. The landlord was not at the inn, and the waiter did not know the stranger's name.

But the next day the man by the window went along to a court case in neighbouring Cork city, for he was very keen on oratory and drama. Once he was seated he noticed the same blue eye and wide forehead in the stout figure in legal robes about to speak.

'My Lurrd – gentlemen of the jury,' spoke the authoritative voice, which was now recognisable.

'Who speaks?' the man instantly whispered.

'Daniel O'Connell,' came the reply.

It was the same Daniel O'Connell that the great French writer Honoré de Balzac would later claim was, along with Napoleon Bonaparte, one of the only great men of the nineteenth century.

It was the same Daniel O'Connell that the once English Prime Minister, William Gladstone, claimed was a 'prophet' who not only did much but 'could not have done more'.

It was the same Daniel O'Connell that the former Irish President Mary Robinson compared to the great civil rights leaders Nelson Mandela and Martin Luther King.

This is the story of Daniel O'Connell.

THE BEST OF YOUTH: 1775–93

Out on the most south-westerly tip of County Kerry, remote and isolated behind Ireland's ten highest mountains, sit the small townlands of Carhen and Derrynane. Some 18 miles apart, the two outposts were once part of 'The O'Connell Country', and both were central to the life of the young Daniel O'Connell.

In the last quarter of the eighteenth century, Daniel's parents, Morgan and Catherine, lived at Carhen, beside the town of Cahirciveen. Catherine (whose maiden name was O'Mullane) hailed from Whitechurch in County Cork, and it was said she was very smart and always cheerful. Morgan was a big, jolly man and was said to be good at backgammon.

3

He was also a businessman, engaged in the manufacture of salt and in leather tanning, and he ran a general store in Cahirciveen.

Having come from Derrynane, where his father owned a substantial amount of land, Morgan struck out independently to settle at Carhen. It was here, in a cottage battered and weathered by Atlantic spray and sea breeze, that the future Liberator was born, on 6 August 1775.

Dan was the first in a family of ten, and he would later boast that the year of his birth coincided with the start of the American War of Independence. This, he said, 'shadowed forth my destiny as a champion of freedom'.

As was common at the time with people of financial means, Dan was fostered out in his youth. He spent the first four years of his life on the mountains of the Iveragh Peninsula in the care of the Cahills, a trusted tenant family on the O'Connell estate.

Dan had a mud cabin for a home, potatoes, milk and fish for food, and the Irish language to communicate with his foster brothers. His foster mother acted as his nurse, while his foster father went out to work every day as a herdsman for the O'Connells.

It was from this fosterage his earliest memory came: in the arms of his nurse, he was rushed to the Kerry coastline where an exciting incident was taking place. The American sailor Paul Jones, in his powerful warship, had come too close to the Irish shore at Valentia harbour. When the ship ran aground in the shallow waters, the crews of two vessels close by were ordered to disembark and fix towing ropes to Jones' ship.

The crew, however, were Irish and English prisoners of war, and they took this opportunity to flee onto dry land. Dan claimed he remembered it all perfectly, with his foster mother beside him, and the wind playing in his golden curls. He marvelled at a tall man astride a grey horse who spat insults at police as they regained control of the prisoners. The scene made a lasting impression on Dan, with this graceful and lone horseman who railed against the authorities, capturing the young boy's imagination.

However, it was Dan's uncle Maurice who would shape him – from

4

youth to middle age – more than any other individual. When Dan, aged five, left the care of his foster family and came down from the mountains, he was, in effect, adopted by Maurice (Morgan's brother), who lived at Derrynane. The inhospitable terrain, and the 18 miles and high mountain pass between Carhen and Maurice's home, meant Dan saw little of his parents in these early days.

Because of the unique velvet headgear Maurice wore, he was known to all as 'Hunting Cap'. His house at Derrynane was large and he ran a considerable estate. He was childless and had resolved to make Dan, who would one day head the O'Connell clan, his heir.

Because of restrictions imposed on Catholics in the form of the Penal Laws, the accumulation of wealth in the late eighteenth century was no easy task. But Hunting Cap had cunning, and he used it, together with south-west Kerry's geographic isolation, to his advantage.

As well as being a landowner, Hunting Cap earned a fortune by smuggling goods from France and Spain. Proper access to Derrynane in the 1770s was restricted to the sea, and so opportunities were considerable for an opportunist and a dodger of the law like Maurice 'Hunting Cap' O'Connell.

Whatever the means, Hunting Cap was in a position to provide the best for Dan, and he was determined to give his nephew a proper education. There was one problem – Dan's natural laziness.

Fortunately, this was matched by something else, which came naturally to the young offspring of Gaelic and Catholic gentry: Dan had an inherent fear of failure and disgrace. And so, with diligence and determination, he persevered. Later in life, he boasted to his great friend William Joseph O'Neill Daunt that he had mastered the alphabet in an hour in these early days.

One evening, at the age of nine, Dan sat brooding in an armchair at Derrynane, where his family had gathered. They were discussing the politician Henry Grattan, and the current affairs of the day. A female relative noted Dan's thoughtful mood. Then, almost as if he had had a vision, the child bullishly announced to the room, 'I'll make a stir in the world yet!'

Outwardly, Dan seemed content and almost too placid. But it was all bluff, and disguised a deep and rich intelligence. He was quick and clever right from the beginning of his schooling. He read voraciously, and passionately held onto Captain Cook's *A Voyage Towards the South Pole*, his first 'big' book. It charted Cook's discovery of new lands in the South Pacific, and it consumed Dan's every thought. He read it, in two great volumes, and re-read it. So passionate was he about the explorer's tales that he would sometimes cry over the stories, clutching the pages to his chest.

Although Cook was one of the British Empire's great seamen and subjects, Britain's dark past was not lost on young Dan. Derrynane held a relic of the worst excesses of English rule in Ireland: on a mantelpiece in the O'Connell house rested the skull of a friar who had been butchered while saying Mass. The clergyman had been scalped at the altar by the sword of a soldier of Oliver Cromwell's army. These gruesome remains were a constant reminder to Dan of the chains in which his fellow countrymen remained shackled.

Hunting Cap was determined that his heir, and hope, would not himself be shackled by these oppressors, and when the Penal Laws were relaxed Dan was sent to an exclusive Catholic school on Long Island, Cork. It was there, under the tutelage of Fr Harrington, that Dan, as one of only twelve boys, spent his first days of formal education.

As the law still didn't allow Catholics (English or Irish) to attend university, Dan was destined to continue his studies on the Continent, where there were a number of excellent schools for Catholics. Aged sixteen, and accompanied by his younger brother, Maurice, he set out for the English College in Liège, Belgium. But the rector of the college quickly rejected the youths on the grounds of their advanced years!

Instead, he sent the pair on to the Holy Trinity in Louvain, which was the prep school for Louvain University. It was a bumpy trip for the

young O'Connells. They did not speak the language, and they had to arrange their own transport. Simply being young Catholics in an area brimming with anti-clerical and anti-Catholic revolution was a test in itself.

On reaching Louvain, the boys soon discovered the courses were too advanced, so they did not attend classes. However, they found hospitality at a monastery of Irish Dominicans, who allowed them the freedom of their library. They larked about, as teenagers tend to do. Needless to say, Hunting Cap would have been livid had he known of the boys' idleness, but they could do little more, as communication with Derrynane took weeks. So the boys waited for the instruction of their uncle, which came finally on 19 October 1791, some six weeks after they had arrived in Louvain. They were to head at once for Saint-Omer in northern France.

At last the boys were to enter the great halls of European education. Saint-Omer excelled in the Classics, notably Greek and Latin, and both English and French were obligatory. The school was designed to produce the complete public man: a man of virtue, honour, intelligence and culture. Its focus on dramatic performance and philosophy might well have been the wellspring for the course of Dan's life.

Hunting Cap was quick to request a personal report on the boys from the school's president, Dr Stapylton. In an extended report on Maurice, the president deemed the younger of the two a sound scholar, 'gentlemanly and much loved by his fellow students'. On Dan, he wrote:

I have but one sentence to write about him - and that is, that I never was so much mistaken in my life as I shall be unless he be destined to make a remarkable figure in society.

Dan himself was determined to be remarkable, so much so that he believed the syllabus was too limited. In a letter to his uncle, he mentioned the English College in Douai and, sure enough, Hunting Cap sent the order to move there. The Continental experience had quickly made a man out of young Dan and once again he had to navigate his way with Maurice through what was, for them, uncharted territory. After borrowing money from Dr Stapylton and an Irish student in Douai, the boys made their way by horse-drawn carriage to that college town, 75 miles east of Saint-Omer. The surroundings at Douai were severe, the food rations meagre, and the boys became increasingly lonely. All this was soon to be overshadowed, however, by the French Revolution.

The Catholic clergy of France were passionately against the Revolution. This meant that Catholic gentry, like the O'Connells, were not safe or welcome in a land increasingly at the mercy of revolutionaries of the lower classes. In September 1792, a mob of the Revolution roamed through Paris and slaughtered scores of Catholic priests, women and children. Twenty-four priests were hacked to death while being transported to prison. The killers wore butchers' aprons as they slashed their way through the victims, covering themselves and everything else in blood. The O'Connell brothers could hear on the wind the thunder of cannon at the Battle of Jemappes, which was not far from Douai. On another occasion, a wagon driver of the Revolutionary Army hurled abuse at them for being Catholics.

The boys realised their time on the Continent was done, and they bolted, this time not waiting for Hunting Cap's approval. They left their belongings to the mercy and profit of the French Republic and fled by horse-drawn carriage for Calais.

The day they left, King Louis XVI had his head severed clean by the guillotine in Paris. During a tense two-day journey west, the boys ran into a group of soldiers who slammed the butts of their rifles against the carriage. Indeed, they were lucky to escape with their lives, and were jeered at as 'little aristocrats' and (wrongly, of course) 'young priests'.

On their cross-country trek, the clever lads wore rosettes in the red, blue and white of the French Republic on their hats, and that might well have saved them. They discarded these false emblems of support once they were safely on board a package liner destined for England. On seeing Dan and Maurice hurling the rosettes into the waters, a group of French fishermen spat an abusive tirade to see them off.

Perhaps it was this early encounter with extremism that convinced Dan such violence, such bloodshed, was no cement for what he would later describe as 'the altar of liberty'.

London, the Law and Learning: 1793–6

From Calais, Dan and Maurice eventually made it to London, where they were taken under the wing of another uncle, Count Daniel Charles. The Count had been a general in the French army, but he too had fled war-torn France for the safer confines of the English capital.

London was initially to be just a stopover for Dan, before a return to Derrynane. He whiled away the time with an old comrade from his schooldays in County Cork, Darby Mahony, who himself was returning from a military campaign with the Irish Brigades. Haymarket was one of their favourite haunts, and they often amused themselves by strolling about the stalls.

Dan, by virtue of his well-heeled background, was never likely to go without, but the strains of constantly having to answer to his strict uncle back at Derrynane must have weighed

11

heavily on his young shoulders. His letters in these days to Hunting Cap, while requesting help, were also grovelling apologies for behaviour that, in truth, was not all that bad.

A month after the two teenagers had been forced to flee France, the Count had to order Dan to seek help from Hunting Cap. Such had been their haste to depart the Continent, the boys had left all their belongings, bar the shirts on their backs, in France. Dan requested some funds from Hunting Cap, but, as always, he closed the letter with meek reassurance to the thrifty chieftain: 'P.S. We are satisfied in every respect with our present situation.'

Hunting Cap wanted the boys to return, but the Count – who had been given his noble title by Louis XVI in 1785 – insisted his nephews be educated in London under his supervision. A friend of Count O'Connell, Chevalier Fagan, agreed to tutor the boys. Unfortunately, due to a lack of numbers attending class, this private schooling lasted only a few months.

Nonetheless, Dan had been a good attendee and took instruction on rhetoric, logic, poetry and philosophy at Fagan's residence. He made good progress, even in this makeshift way, and the Count assured Hunting Cap in December 1793 that his nephews were 'improved in their carriage and demeanour. Dan is promising everything that is good and estimable.'

Young Maurice, on the other hand, fell out of favour with his uncles for an unknown breach. The legal profession, for which Dan was destined, was not something Maurice was willing to entertain. His wish was to become a soldier, and that left the clan little choice but to take him out of London.

By that Christmas, Dan, too, had begun to get itchy feet, and home-sickness set in. Citing a litany of reasons why Dublin would be a more fitting hub for his education, he tried to convince Hunting Cap to let him return to Ireland. Alas, his attempts foundered, and by the end of the following month he had enrolled as a law student at Lincoln's Inn in London. It was here that he took his first step on the road to public life.

From his lodgings on the Strand, he set about preparing himself as best he could for his imminent education at the Bar. His best course of action from that January would have been to go under the wing of a barrister. This would be hands-on work experience, but the £100 annual fee was beyond Dan's reach. He never told Hunting Cap of this option, fearing the wrath of the old miser. Reading was the only course of action for a young man of his means, and William Blackstone's *Commentaries on the Laws of England* took up much of his spare time. Dan's interest in oration was also beginning to take shape and he began to study history and literature of high quality, which provide that strength and solidity that every public speaker needs.

Maurice finally left his brother's side in March 1794, taking flight with Darby back to Kerry. Hunting Cap's chosen heir was now alone in the English metropolis. In a letter home, he mentioned his lack of social activity. He had not gone, he claimed morosely to his uncle, 'to one single place of public entertainment since I came to London'. A further setback came in

August when Dan suffered from an acute sickness and what he described as 'slow nervous fever'. He took nearly a month to recover.

He had perked up sufficiently in October to attend and study the treason trials of Thomas Hardy and John Horne Tooke at the Old Bailey. Hardy and Tooke were what was known as 'radicals' and had been agitating for reform of the system of government. In Dan's mind their suppression and trial had been a great injustice and was evidence that the Government, led by Prime Minister William Pitt, was bent on silencing the voice of the people. The charges were eventually dropped and both men were freed, but the trial left an impression on Dan. In the words of his son John, speaking years later of his father's attendance at the trials, 'the process of change in his mind ended by converting him to popular opinions, and confirming his natural detestation of tyranny'.

At the time of the trials Dan was boarding in Coventry Street. Many years later, while passing by his former residence and adjacent fishmongers, he

recalled to a friend: 'That shop is in precisely the same state in which I remember it when I was at Gray's Inn nearly fifty years ago – the same sized window, the same frontage; I believe, the same fish!'

The art of oration and the fine delivery of speech was part of the armoury of any public man in the late eighteenth century. Dan, now an ambitious nineteen-year-old, had already joined the Society of Cogers. It was at this gentlemen's debating society that he began to hone his skills as a public speaker. On a field trip in early 1795 he attended a famous debate at the House of Commons. Pitt, the Prime Minister, was up against the Whig MP Charles James Fox. Although Dan disagreed with Pitt's form of government, the Prime Minister's speaking skills left a more favourable impression. He thought Pitt's oratory was superb, not just in volume and flow, but in the way he managed his voice:

'He threw his voice so completely around the House that every syllable he uttered was distinctly heard by every man in the House.'

This was to be a great lesson for Dan, and a skill that he would master in the years ahead.

Though determined to make it in the world, Dan was, nonetheless, not completely averse to the hedonistic ways of youth. On Sunday 26 April 1795 he tipped along to the Packhorse Tavern in Chiswick. 'A bottle', as he had suggested to his friend Richard Newton Bennett, turned into a day's drinking. In the course of the evening they were joined by two more friends, Douglas Thompson and De Vignier. 'De V.' was often a fright when he was drunk, and on this occasion he duly tormented a young lady before Dan and Bennett dragged him away.

Later, in the street, De V. knocked on several doors in search of juvenile amusement. He had not bargained on the challenge posed from the door of a Mr de Faria, a Portuguese landlord. His servant, Mr Middleton, stepped out and challenged the young men to a fight, to which Dan obliged.

'We made some blows at each other without effect, when De V. rushed at my antagonist and kicked him in the belly,' Dan would later recall.

The servant held his own and struck the onrushing Bennett in the face, before the latter composed himself and paid Middleton back in spades.

The daughters of de Faria, as well as the man himself, rushed from the house and proceeded to pummel Bennett, before our three heroes attempted to make a hasty escape. They were apprehended on the street by a constable, and suddenly half the district was out watching the young men being escorted to a police station. Dan, somewhat the worse for wear, proceeded to hurl abuse at de Faria. The trio of Dan, Bennett and De V. spent the night in the police station under a guard's close scrutiny, licking their wounds and waiting to face the morning.

That summer Dan got a welcome break from the London metropolis and made his way to Derrynane for the first time in almost four years. He would later recall with sadness those last days spent on the Iveragh Peninsula with Darby Mahony. His close friend would soon perish on a mission in the West Indies. He resolved, in Darby's memory, 'as life is short, to endeavour to be as happy as I can. I will make my heart a heart of love; that, and that alone, is the way to be happy'.

In late October Dan returned to London, where he discovered his rent in the middle of town had risen considerably. This was due primarily to the French Revolution, still raging across the English Channel. Hunting Cap gave the order to move house and seek lodgings farther out of town. Bennett was again on hand and Dan soon moved in with his ally at the residence of a Mrs Rigby. He assured his uncle that all was well at his new abode: 'The society in the house are people of rank and knowledge of the world; so that their conversation and manners are perfectly well adapted to rub off the rust of scholastic education.'

The truth might have been less welcome to Hunting Cap. As Dan noted in his personal diary, the house was run in a scattershot manner, by a lady of questionable morals.

'Her faculties are cultivated by an almost universal study,' wrote Dan around Christmas 1795, but equally, 'she is deficient in common decorum and cleanliness.'

He painted a picture of a house full of high minds, cats and a particularly bohemian matriarch who had a penchant for alcohol: 'In her attachment for cats she becomes foolish and absurd. She gets drunk sometimes and when heated with drinking she is rude in her familiarities.'

It was in these heady days that Dan began to familiarise himself more with the young ladies of London, and on one occasion brought two city types with him to a large party in Hammersmith. As the night was coming to a close, he went to retrieve one of his companions, a Ms King, who was

in mid-conversation with his friend Douglas Thompson. Thompson was not particularly happy and a quarrel ensued. Dan assured him he had behaved 'in a rascally manner, and you shall hear about it'.

The next morning, while at breakfast, Dan received a letter from Thompson demanding an explanation as to why he had been called a 'rascal'. Such correspondence was the first step in requesting a duel. A duel usually required a 'second', someone to act on one's behalf. However, as his newly-wed friend Richard Newton Bennett was away, Dan marched to Thompson's residence himself. After a verbal altercation at the door, Thompson retreated inside where he grabbed his cane and quickly began to lash out at Dan, who held back, reasoning that he was a much bigger man, with a much heavier cane.

When word got out about the incident, the Count chastised Dan for his folly, and wondered aloud why his young nephew had returned to

Chiswick – the place where Thomson was living, and the scene of his previous altercation outside the Packhorse. Dan, though, took some solace from the knowledge that, unlike previously, he had not stooped to the indignity of street fighting: 'I reflect with pleasure on the courage which I felt on this occasion. All I have to fear is precipitation in plunging myself in future quarrels.'

While he learned from experience, Dan was also becoming more and more philosophical. His wide reading at this time was enhanced by argument and late-night debate at Mrs Rigby's. Much of his thinking was based on the eminent writers of the day, such as William Godwin and Thomas Paine.

'His work cannot be too highly praised,' wrote Dan of Godwin's *Political Justice*, which argued that individual human reason, rather than oppressive government control, should decide the best course of action for all. Equally, Paine's *The Age of Reason* promoted logic and freethinking above the authority and constraints of religious institutions. These texts, published in the midst of a revolution and radical in thought, were the kind a student, and a Catholic outsider, could easily trumpet as the voice of a new age.

Dan began to abhor the death penalty, and most likely based his case on the theories of Paine's *Rights of Man*. His position hardened in January 1796 when he attended the trial and sentencing of two young men found guilty of robbing the occupants of a horse-drawn carriage.

'If these unfortunate individuals are hanged,' wrote Dan, 'will one more virtue be infused into the bosom of any individual? Will one crime less be committed than would be had they escaped? Certainly not.'

Also, in an age when women were viewed merely as instruments for providing children and succour for the menfolk, Dan held more radical views. After reading Mary Wollstonecraft's *A Vindication of the Rights of Woman*, he reflected that 'mind has no sex. Surely the judgement of the one sex ought to be as unshackled as that of the other.'

In the late spring of 1796, Dan was ready to return to Ireland to complete his studies. While just twenty years of age, his radical thoughts and ideas were already becoming concrete. His travels had given him independence of spirit and of mind. He was a young adult about to become fully fledged.

DUBLIN, TONE AND THE 1798 REBELLION: 1796–9

'I am now, as it were, arrived at a new stage of my life.'

Just days after arriving back in Dublin in the middle of May 1796, approaching his twenty-first birthday, Dan assured Hunting Cap he was ready to begin afresh. He took a room at 22 Stafford Street, where he paid a guinea a week for board and lodging. It was ideally situated to complete the final term of the academic year, being just a stone's throw from the law college of the King's Inns. Not that attending lectures – nor, for that matter, passing exams – was necessary. The only training Dan was compelled to do was sit through a number of dinners in Hall. This in itself would, supposedly, ensure enough intellectual enlightenment by way of the highbrow conversation legal students were assumed to have while dining.

Yet, however much he tried to hide the fact from his uncle, Dan was homesick, and that summer he returned eagerly to his old stomping ground in the south-west. A sharp intellect, and bookish maybe, he was nonetheless always an outdoorsman. One morning during this carefree season he decided to go gallivanting around Kerry on Hunting Cap's favourite horse, albeit without his uncle's permission.

Dan struck for Kilrelig, stopping off to hunt for hares, and then headed on to Bolus Head to see the otter caves. He slept rough, as was his habit on these mini-expeditions. He was in his element as he rode on north to Tarmon, where he went fox hunting, before decamping to a wedding at Direen.

20

Dan later wrote that he had many happy moments during the year, but also many miserable ones, most notably when he fell out with Hunting Cap for taking his prized horse. The letter Dan received from his brother in November cannot have helped matters. Maurice, finally about to follow his own path in a soldier's uniform, wrote to him from the deck of the *Middleton Transport*, after setting out from Waterford harbour:

My Dear Dan,

I am with a worthy honest set of lads, Capt O'Connor commanding,

going we know not where but it is imagined up the Mediterranean.

Our instructions will be opened at sea.

Dearest brother, adieu and best of friends, adieu perhaps forever.

Maurice's conclusion was prophetic. He served for only a year; his young life ended when he succumbed to yellow fever while posted at Santo Domingo in the Caribbean.

And yet, no matter how comfortable things were for Dan at end of 1796, he began to feel bored with his lot, however occupied his reading was keeping him. The mammoth *The Decline and Fall of the Roman Empire* by Edward Gibbon, as well as John Whitaker's *The History of Manchester*, engaged his time at the Dublin Library on Eustace Street, but already Dan seemed to yearn for an active role in the theatre of the world. Alas, his reading was not enough:

'My life, though it is not in any degree insipid, is monotonous and unchequered.'

Not even the drinks supped at an inn around this time with his friends Marshall, Bland and Fuller could lift Dan's weariness: 'I was not by any means intoxicated, nor was I much amused.'

Only days after this particular night of monotony, however, events began that would greatly spark his interest. The previous February, a certain Irishman, named James Smith, had been making his way through Normandy, on his way to Paris. He had witnessed first-hand the positive results that could arise when people united against an oppressive regime to claim their rights. 'Smith' – a ruse to mask his real name, Wolfe Tone – had helped found the Society of United Irishmen in 1791. The society (soon declared illegal) had been inspired by the French Revolution, and its initial aims were parliamentary reform and the removal of English control over Irish affairs. Tone himself was a radical, however, and he wanted more than reform; he wanted to sever the connection completely. He had long believed that 'the bane of Irish prosperity' was 'the influence of England'. He concluded that 'that influence will ever be exerted while the connection between the countries continues'.

Tone knew that connection could be broken with the help of the French, who were themselves at war with England. He had been in France to outline to the new regime, the French Directory, how, through Ireland, they could defeat their mutual enemy. By a remarkable blend of perseverance and persuasion, Tone – considered the father of Irish republicanism – had made many useful contacts with French ministers of foreign affairs and war. Now, in December 1796, he, together with the great French general Lazare Hoche, was heading a fleet of warships towards Bantry in County Cork. Among the first to spot the ships was Dan's first cousin, Daniel O'Sullivan, who broke the news with an urgent letter to Hunting Cap:

My Dear Uncle,
We are in the greatest uneasiness here on account of the French fleet, which are turning up Bantry Bay.

When word reached Dan in Dublin he was equally uneasy at the prospects. 'I know the victories of the French would be attended with bad consequences,' he wrote from his lodgings.

As the hordes on the street anticipated a French-style revolution of their own, Dan condemned such an action. In a candlelit room, he put his quill to paper:

The Irish people are not yet sufficiently enlightened to be able to bear the sun of freedom ... They would rob, they would murder.

23

The altar of liberty totters when it is cemented only with blood, when it is supported only with carcasses.

The prospect of a military invasion by the French aided and abetted by one of his own generation – Tone – only hardened Dan's belief that liberty should be sought and won by the hands of peace: 'The liberty I look for is that which would increase the happiness of mankind.'

Dan was only twenty-one, but the road ahead was already chosen: 'In the service of this liberty I have devoted my life and whatever portion of talents I may have or acquire.'

As it happened, a tempest at sea held the fleet from landing. On Christmas Day, aboard the *Indomitable*, under the alias 'Adjutant-general Smith', Tone wandered the ship's deck muttering to himself: 'I am devoured by the most gloomy reflections. The wind continues right ahead, so that it is absolutely impossible to work up to the landing place, and God knows when it will change.'

Four days later the expedition was called off. Defeated by the wind, the fleet pulled anchor and steered home for France.

While Dan had condemned the whole incident, it had, nonetheless, stirred his passion for adventure. He saw much in the world of combat to loathe, but there was much esteem to be earned, too, by donning a military uniform. Nothing would do him now but to join the Lawyers' Corps of the Yeomanry, a volunteer unit of the British army used to quell riots and civil disturbances. Perhaps out of fear of Hunting Cap's fury (correctly, as it turned out), Dan signed up behind his uncle's back. Hunting Cap, when he discovered the truth, initially refused to allow his eager nephew enter service.

And so Dan stomped about in a frenzy of youthful disappointment, and in one exaggerated outburst even threatened to take his own life. Eventually his pleading won the day and Hunting Cap relented. Free from the need to sulk, Dan now looked forward to the honour of wearing a serviceman's uniform: 'The recollection of having been in a volunteer corps will hereafter be pleasant. It will still be more pleasant to be always able to say, "I was a volunteer."'

His training was not particularly challenging, but he did learn how to march and handle artillery. He was proud to look and feel like a soldier.

It was also at this time that Dan became overwhelmed by another great distraction – a young lady by the name of Eliza. 'Sweet Eliza', as his first mention of her read, on Saturday 14 January 1797, filled his passions so completely it briefly threatened his ruin. Infatuated, and sick with emotion, he wept over his diary. The following Wednesday he afforded her much more than two words, gushing poetically:

Eliza, let my love for thee mingle in the cup of my sorrows. There must, assuredly there must be an exquisite pleasure in madness. Would I was mad! Then, Eliza, I would rave of thee; then should I forget my uncle's tyranny.

Yet, with the whim of youth, Dan quickly decided to drop her, and even scoffed at the notion of commitment:

How blind are unfortunate mortals to their defects? Eliza imagined that she had made an impression on me!

Batting away his youthful folly, Dan quickly turned his attentions to loftier matters.

On 28 January he considered 'the plan to be pursued when I come into Parliament' – and this at a time when Catholics were not even permitted as Members! While he admitted to being often 'led away by vanity and ambition', Dan also had a strange sense of his destiny: 'Distant prospects rise unrequested to my sight. They are not unwelcome to my heart.'

In February, he visited the Irish House of Commons, where he heard a speech by Sir Lawrence Parsons. The address, on defending Ireland's shores, did not impress Dan, and he was also disappointed with the speaker's poor oratorical style. Indeed, he dismissed the poor standard of most Members sitting in Parliament.

'I too will be a Member,' Dan vowed at once. 'Young as I am, unacquainted with the ways of the world ... I will steadfastly attach myself to the real interests of Ireland.'

His determination to succeed was prone to interruption by great moments of anguish, railing at the constraints of the corrupt political system. As a law student with increasing awareness of his ability, Dan also knew that the highest levels of the profession were cut off from him, as a Catholic. He was now in the Yeomanry, yet the Establishment it was designed to protect was daily increasing its persecution of his people. Only two years previously, on 5 May 1795, a bill to admit Catholics to the Irish House of Commons had been rejected by a majority of more than three to one. Dan's aspirations in 1797, for all their ambition, were no more than a distant dream.

'It was a terrible time,' he recalled in later life. 'The political leaders of the period could not conceive such a thing as a perfectly open and above board political machinery.'

His duty in volunteering with the Lawyers' Corps did not prevent him from supporting the nationalist cause.

'I was myself a United Irishman,' he said at the age of sixty. Such was the ferment of the time, had he spoken this aloud in 1797 he would, in all probability, have been hanged. Not even a supposed ally could be trusted on the eve of the 1798 Rebellion, and so Dan's movements in these days are shrouded in secrecy. He was afraid of men who wanted to be rebels on the one hand, but were petrified on the other by the risk of hanging.

Dan attended a meeting of a reformers' club at a tavern on Eustace Street around this time. Much as his passions were stoked, he never spoke up, and left the debating to other, more violent men. Years later he would

26

reflect with some relief that he had remained a silent onlooker, such were the dire consequences of speaking out against the Government at the time. Dan's legal career, for one thing, would have been in jeopardy. The Chancellor, John FitzGibbon, was the strong arm of Government repression – he had the highest judicial and political office in the country – and took a hard line on student insurrection. He punished a politically radical law student by postponing his qualification, and would soon lead a purge of Trinity College, expelling nineteen scholars who were supposed members of the United Irishmen.

'A great deal of the misery of man can clearly be derived from the form of government under which he lives,' Dan wrote on 24 March 1797. Although the threat of severe punishment hung over him, his morals were not to be compromised: 'I love liberty – I love liberty as conducive to increase the portion of human happiness.'

The United Irishmen in Dublin decided to display their strength in numbers at two funeral processions that April. The first, for an Edward Dunn, was attended by over 5,000 well-drilled men who wore green handkerchiefs and ribbons. It was a show of nationalism that intensified when some militiamen joined the procession. Dan and his friend Richard Newton Bennett attended the second funeral, that of a millwright named Ryan. Again the assembly was packed. Dan, along with Bennett, was alleged to have stirred up some of the crowd by asking them to help to raid cannon from the Lawyers' Corps yard to arm the United Irishmen. Trouble rose up all over Dublin and martial law was declared. A curfew was imposed. The Duke of Leinster, a supporter of Catholic Emancipation, resigned in protest.

The day after the 'famous funeral', Dan declared solemnly:

'We are probably at the eve of a great change in administration.'

He would later tear out pages of his journal from this time, May 1797, perhaps wary of prosecution over radical entries.

27

The following month, Dan set off for Derrynane and spent a long holiday far removed from the bubbling volcano of revolution. Fishing and hunting took up much of his time, and he did not arrive back in the capital until November. He believed he had misspent his time during the summer, and had done very little better since his return to Dublin. He resolved to throw everything at his final term as a law student, stating he was never more firmly intent upon anything.

Although distracted by his reading, Dan was, nevertheless, caught up in the fervour of a country on the cusp of outright rebellion. As sectarian divisions deepened, Chancellor FitzGibbon increased his support of Catholic persecution. Dan spoke out vehemently while at a dinner party in March 1798. Influenced by too much wine perhaps, he called for a prayer book to swear in some zealous young men as United Irishmen. The host, a cheesemonger by the name of Murray, tried to deter him from further rash outbursts, but to little effect. On his way home that night Dan went to the aid of a man being beaten by a gang of thugs. After getting the better of three of the attackers, Dan was seized from behind and savagely beaten. Forced to bed with his injuries, he was advised by Matthew Regan, his landlord, on the folly of speaking out politically at such a time.

Regan's point had merit, as that same month Dan's name appeared on a list of radicals operating in Dublin. Francis Higgins, also known as 'The Sham Squire', was a notorious conman and informant, and it was he who penned a dubious report mixing Dan up with his uncle, the Count. In the report, he accused Dan of receiving a letter from the son of James Napper Tandy (a radical patriot and United Irishman). Tandy was planning anarchy from his exile in France, and now Higgins was attempting to connect Dan with this potential unrest. He may have been spied upon, but the charge against Dan was flimsy and no action was taken.

When martial law was declared on the streets, the Yeomanry was called to arms. Its reckless violence against Catholics was well established, but Dan was one of a tiny minority of his religion in the regiment. He was posted on duty on one of Dublin's canal bridges. On one occasion, he flatly refused an order to fire on some unarmed people from the country who were breaking curfew. On another occasion, he caught the slash of a sword on his musket when he came between an irate colleague and an unarmed civilian. The ensuing fight between the two Yeomen was only broken up when a sergeant arrived on the scene.

As Dan said himself at the time, the odium against the Catholics was 'becoming every day more deep-rooted'. On the eve of the 1798 Rebellion, 19 May, he was given some relief from the increasingly hostile climate when he was formally called to the Bar. That month he took a small number of cases to open his legal career, but the court season was cut short due to the outbreak of the Rebellion. Many of the roads around the country had been closed off due to the unrest, so in early June Dan struck for Kerry aboard a potato boat that sailed around the Irish coast.

Many people were dying in the insurrection, with hundreds falling in places like the Curragh in County Kildare and Tara Hill in County Meath.

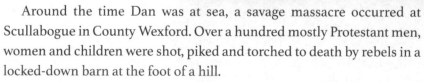

Around the time Dan was at sea, a savage massacre occurred at Scullabogue in County Wexford. Over a hundred mostly Protestant men, women and children were shot, piked and torched to death by rebels in a locked-down barn at the foot of a hill.

Outrages like Scullabogue were carried out by both the Government and rebels over the next four months. The King's men gained decisive

29

victories in Wexford, Longford and Donegal, at Vinegar Hill, Ballinamuck and, ultimately, Tory Island. The Battle of Tory Island saw Wolfe Tone again attempt an attack with a French fleet, only to be overpowered by the British navy. That was to be the final action of the 1798 Rebellion.

With land communication shut down during the insurrection, and being in the deep isolation of Derrynane, Dan had been at a complete remove from the storm of upheaval. Although he was away from the troubles of the nation, he suffered a personal malady that would have a lasting effect on him. While out hunting on the hills, he got soaked in a downpour, and took to a peasant's hut for shelter. He sat in front of the glowing hearth, and after enjoying a bottle of whiskey he fell asleep in his wet clothes. The next morning, he awoke to face the day and resume the hunt. He was soon overcome with fatigue, however, and fell asleep in a ditch under a scorching sun. He became feverish, and later recalled, 'I spent a fortnight in great discomfort, wandering about and unable to eat.' Finally, no longer able battle it out, he gave up and went to bed.

A local doctor, Moriarty, was sent for, and soon diagnosed the fever. Dan was convinced he was going to die, and claimed he felt his backbone 'stiffening for death'. He became delirious, and imagined he was in the middle of a wood, and that the branches were on fire around him.

Under the doctor's care, he gradually regained his strength, and towards the latter part of his illness he listened while Moriarty talked about Napoleon Bonaparte's descent on Alexandria. The doctor assured the young man that Napoleon had led his entire army across the desert.

'Impossible!' retorted Dan. 'He cannot have done so; they would have starved.'

When Moriarty said it was thanks to a large quantity of portable soup that they survived, Dan replied, 'Had they portable water? For their portable soup would have been of little use if they had not water to dissolve it in.' At this, Moriarty turned to Dan's mother, Catherine, and assured her, 'His intellect, at any rate, is untouched.'

At last, in November of that nightmarish year, Dan returned to Dublin. It was at this time, in the same city, that Wolfe Tone committed suicide in order to avoid the hangman's noose. At the end of this *annus horribilis*, Dan reflected on the worst of times when he met up with Newton Bennett:

'We talked much of the late unhappy rebellion. A great deal of blood was shed on the occasion. Good God!'

Remembering the accounts of Vinegar Hill and Scullabogue, Dan later wrote in his diary:

Oh, Liberty, what horrors are perpetrated in thy name! May every virtuous revolutionist remember the horrors of Wexford!

As a new future lay in wait for the country, Dan, too, resolved to move on from a year that was 'wretchedly misspent'.

Dan and the Law: 1798–1830

After recovering from the fever that had nearly killed him in 1798, Dan was determined to resume his legal career. The bookish young man was about to practise law on the Munster circuit. This meant spending five or six weeks travelling the rough roads and byways between the assizes of Ennis, Limerick, Tralee and Cork. In the late eighteenth century the rugged and mountainous landscape of south-west Ireland was wild and undeveloped. The trek from district to district by mail coach, carriage or on horseback was a real hardship.

'If anything were capable of destroying my natural vitality it would be those infernal mountains and roads,' Dan would later reflect.

One early morning in 1799 he set out on these roads on his first circuit, leaving Carhen on horseback at four o'clock. His brother John accompanied him for some time, but once they had reached the

32

mountains they parted ways, with John turning off to go hare hunting.

'How I did envy him,' said Dan, 'whilst *I* had to enter on the drudgery of my profession.'

As the sun came up, his mood lightened, and he was soon making a hard trot for Tralee, where he arrived at noon. There, he fed and rested his horse and recuperated briefly, before setting off again for Tarbert. A few hours later, after he had passed Listowel, clouds blackened the sky and a downpour forced him to shelter under a bridge.

An eminent local gentleman, also escaping the deluge, then emerged. They greeted each other, before the gentleman asked Dan where he had come from, and why he had been on the road so late. In a time when most people did not travel outside their own district, the revelation that he had been travelling for close on twelve hours shocked his inquisitor:

'*You'll do*,' he chuckled, praising the young Dan, 'I see, *you'll do*.'

When the rain eased Dan remounted and struck for Tarbert. At five o'clock in the late afternoon, and after a journey of some 60 miles, he and his steed finally arrived in the north Kerry town. Tired as he was, he still dreaded having to spend the evening alone at an inn that did not even have a book for distraction: 'I had no acquaintance in the town; and I felt my spirits low enough at the prospects of a long, stupid evening.'

By chance, his old friend Ralph Marshall was in Tarbert the same evening and they bumped into each other at the inn. Marshall was off to a ball, and after a little convincing Dan was soon in tow, and spent the night dancing. He finally got to bed at 2 a.m., and rose only hours later to start out for the Limerick assizes.

It was natural enough that Dan would pick Munster as his circuit of choice, as not only did he hail from Kerry, but he had several relations throughout the province. It was in his home county, in the town of Tralee, that he made his first big mark on circuit. He was a junior barrister on this initial tour of Munster. His low rank meant that if called upon to question a witness, he could pass the duty over to a senior, as most juniors did. But when it fell upon Dan to do the questioning, he was not the man to dodge the challenge: 'I thought it due to myself to attempt it, hit or miss!'

Dan started by humouring 'Darby', the witness in question.

'You are a good-humoured, honest fellow,' he began. He then asked if Darby had 'taken a drop of anything that day?'

'Your honour, I took my share of a pint of spirits,' came the reply.

Dan reminded Darby he was under oath, and so forced the witness to admit that 'his share' had been the entire contents. This created a 'general and hearty laugh' in the courtroom, after which the witness stood down. If the man was drunk on the day in question his evidence could not be relied upon. Dan had won his point, and had announced his arrival on the scene. Even if he was a junior, he gained much respect during his first circuit.

Young Dan's wide reading had already made him well versed in the technicalities of law, but for a Catholic to succeed in a profession dominated by Protestants he needed to become the greatest of legal experts. Though he became a barrister in 1798, he did not yet have a complete grasp of all aspects of law. He vowed that by 1800 he would be an expert in all forms. This determination drove him to become not only an expert but, as one barrister of the day put it, 'the best criminal lawyer in Europe'.

Restrictions on Catholics meant he could not rise as high in his profession as a Protestant. This made Dan bitter at times. Indeed, he showed outright and open contempt for judges on many occasions. Supposedly his superiors, Dan knew many held their positions not on merit, but by virtue of their Ascendancy background.

On one occasion, at the Cork assizes, the judge would not let him call a witness. Dan argued that he was legally entitled to do so, but the judge argued otherwise. The court ruled against Dan and the witness was not allowed to give evidence. The next morning the trial resumed, by which time the judge had consulted his legal textbooks.

'I have reconsidered my decision of yesterday,' said the judge. 'My present opinion is that the evidence tendered by you should not have been rejected. You can therefore produce the evidence now,' he instructed Dan. Another lawyer might have been grateful to have his evidence heard, no matter how late in the day, but not Dan.

'Had your lordship known as much law yesterday morning as you do today,' snapped Dan, 'you would have spared me a vast amount of time and trouble, and my client a considerable amount of injury. Call up the witness!' The injury was now with the judge, who shrank in embarrassed silence.

Other judges, too, were assessed with equal venom. Judge Toler, according to Dan, was 'ridiculous' and nothing but a 'pretty gentleman'. Dan referred to Toler simply as 'The Thing'. Judge Arthur Wolfe's 'pompous inanity' was 'insufferable', while Judge Fox was 'morose, sour and impetuous'.

Dan saved a story for his friend O'Neill Daunt, about Judge Boyd, a 'drunkard'. Boyd had been seen sucking on a quill that sat among the pens in an inkstand on his desk. The 'inkstand' was full of brandy. As it happened, on the day in question a witness was cross-examined about whether he had been drunk on the night of an incident.

'Come now, my good man,' said Judge Boyd to the witness, 'tell the court truly, were you drunk or were you sober upon that occasion?'

'Oh, quite sober,' intervened the witness's lawyer, Mr Harry Grady, who stood glaring at the inkstand – 'as sober *as a judge*.'

On occasion, Dan used the incompetence of many of his colleagues to his advantage, belittling opponents with insults and vexed rants. It was all part of his armoury. On one occasion, Dan's aggressive tactics inside the courtroom almost resulted in a duel. In a bid to prosecute a Mr Segerson for assault, Dan began to insult him. Segerson erupted, jumped up and called Dan 'a purse-proud blockhead'. Dan replied, 'If I be a blockhead, it is better for you, as I am against you.'

But then Dan did something foolish. He grabbed a cane close by and whacked Segerson on the back. The next day, Segerson proposed a duel, but quickly backed down when he discovered Dan was financing him by renting some of his land.

'I cannot afford to shoot you,' cried Segerson, 'unless ... you first insure your life for my benefit. If you do, then I'm your man.'

Dan believed him to be a coward and found the whole incident 'so ludicrously absurd'. He may have had himself to blame for the 'absurd' incident, but these trifles happened rarely, and Dan was blessed with both personal and physical advantages. As one barrister who witnessed Dan in court put it: 'Dan was a fine, well-developed figure, clear blue eye, features expressive of keen intelligence, and a voice of great power, now rolling like tones of a grand organ, bursting forth in thunder, then dying away into deep pathos, rushing into rapid speech, or, if engaged in denunciation, pouring forth epithets strong, fierce and stinging.'

Dan's skill at cross-examination was one of his greatest strengths, and it was used brilliantly in the case against a Kerry smuggler. The south-west of Ireland – particularly the peninsulas of Cork and Kerry, which jut into the Atlantic – was a haven for outlaws and smugglers of contraband. Around 1820, a time when poverty ravaged the country, illegal activity around the coastal bays and inlets was so rampant the Government was hard pressed to stamp it out.

Officials in Dublin sent an officer to Dingle with orders to seize offenders and bring them to trial. The officer sent was a Mr Flood, who had, at one time, occupied a lowly position in the Crow Street Theatre in Dublin. He was a colourful character, prone to enacting great scenes from dramas of the day. He was also noted for mimicking many fine actors of the stage, much to the amusement of those who happened to be in his company.

While posted in Dingle he did not so much enjoy his spare time as completely neglect his duty. Putting on impromptu plays for the youths of the district, he soon became the main man in a small drama society. Flood lapped up his new popularity, and partook of grand suppers that followed these plays and private theatricals. Though fowl was particularly scarce, there was no shortage on these festive occasions, and Flood 'was not over particular how they were procured'. The bounty of fowl was a result of the ransacking of hen roosts and poultry yards.

Word reached Dublin of Flood's escapades in the south-west. He was informed he would be dismissed if he did not soon produce some results in his professional duties. As luck would have it, a huge cargo of illegal tobacco sat anchored off the Kerry coast, and when a notorious smuggler named Connor attempted to offload it, Flood was there to apprehend him. The capture of forty horses, each weighed down by three large bales of tobacco, was so significant it got Flood off the hook with his superiors.

Connor was held in jail while he awaited trial at the Tralee assizes. It was expected he would be found guilty, with fourteen years' transportation the likely outcome. Connor's family immediately called upon Dan's services.

On the morning of the trial, the accused's friends tried to help Dan, and ruin the case against Connor, by plying Flood with alcohol. Clearly the worse for wear on the stand, Flood still managed to describe accurately how he captured Connor and the smuggled goods. As Flood got up to leave the witness stand, Dan called out, 'Come back, Alonzo.' It was a reference to a part Flood had once played, and Dan immediately had his attention.

'*Alonzo the Brave and the Fair Imogene*,' sighed Flood, reminiscing with a smile.

'And who was your Imogene in Dingle?' joked Dan, as he went on to enquire about the theatricals Flood had been part of. Dan eventually asked about the suppers – the geese, turkeys, chickens and all the other fowl that had been stolen, slaughtered and enjoyed by Flood and his posse.

Flood lost his temper, and, with the alcohol consumed doing him no favours, he began to contradict himself. Such was his confusion that he launched into more theatrics.

'My love, my life, my Belvidera!' he cried, much to the amusement of all. He attempted to embrace Dan, but promptly fell off the stand. In the babble of a confused courtroom, the jury took only a few minutes of deliberation before acquitting Connor, reasoning that Flood was a very unreliable witness. Dan later described this unlikely victory as his greatest triumph in a court of justice.

While he defended many questionable characters, Dan was seldom upset when he lost a case of particular brutality. In March 1820, he defended John Scanlan over a charge of murder. However, the evidence against Scanlan was so strong that Dan, when he lost the case, did not feel even a slight regret at his client's conviction.

Scanlan was of the gentry, and had eloped with Ellen Hanley, a fifteen-year-old peasant girl. He quickly came to regret their marriage. He robbed his new bride of what little she had, and then murdered her while on a boat trip, with the help of a servant, Michael Sullivan. Young Ellen was thrown overboard in the estuary of the River Shannon; her body washed up at Moneypoint in County Clare some months later.

Suspicions quickly arose after the fatal boat trip, because Scanlan kept changing the story of his young wife's whereabouts. When fishermen eventually discovered the body, everything pointed to Scanlan and Sullivan, who had both been seen wearing items of jewellery belonging to Ellen in the aftermath of the disappearance.

By the time of the trial the scandal had piqued the public imagination, and sympathy was firmly with the young victim. Dan's chances of a successful defence were not good. Evidence was mounting against the accused, and it was impossible for Dan to beat down the facts. Scanlan was found guilty and publicly hanged. Sullivan was tried later and condemned to the same fate.

'It is very unusual for me to be so satisfied,' said Dan, 'but Scanlan is a horrid villain.' With dark interest, Dan would later read, and enjoy, books inspired by this national scandal: the novel *The Collegians* and a play called *The Colleen Bawn*. Dan's courtroom days were all but over in the summer of 1829. By that stage he had stepped away from his profession and into the world of politics. But while resting at Derrynane after a tough year, Dan was called upon to defend the lives of close to two dozen of the townsfolk of Doneraile in County Cork.

Only six months previously the carriage of a local doctor, John Norcott, had been fired upon by members of the Whiteboys, a secret oath-bound society. They had mistaken Norcott for Michael Creagh, a local landlord who was particularly despised. Following this attempted assassination, plans were set in motion to kill other unpopular landlords and magistrates in the area.

Throughout the 1820s there had been a number of Whiteboy disturbances in north Cork, and Doneraile sat in the middle of an area of particular unrest. Attacks and raids on Big Houses, as well as widespread burning of property, had terrorised the Protestant gentry. The Establishment wanted to put down this violence, and with the help of spies and bribed informers they eventually rounded up twenty-two Catholic peasants whom they intended to hang – whether guilty or not of the attempted assassination. To make a point, the Government sent the Solicitor General, John Doherty, to Cork to lead the case against the accused.

On Friday 23 October 1829, four of the prisoners had been tried and found guilty, after just twenty minutes of deliberation by the jury. The four, including seventy-year-old John Leary, were sentenced to hang. But to the public, these convictions were immediately seen as a glaring miscarriage of justice. The local people had expected the defendants to be acquitted.

39

To save the lives of the remaining eighteen men, something drastic needed to be done.

The Crown's prosecution, in Doherty, was proving too strong for the defence of a Mr McCarthy and a Mr Pigott. So the prisoners' relatives decided only one man could match Doherty – Daniel O'Connell. Dan's parliamentary career was, at this stage, about to take off (as we shall see in Chapter 12) and he was now taking a well-earned break in Derrynane. It was a 90-mile trek from Doneraile, but the locals there were determined to get their man.

With thirty-six hours to spare until the next court hearing on the Monday morning, William Burke, a brother of one of the prisoners, set out on horseback. He travelled throughout the night on unknown roads through the black and silent countryside. His mare was close to collapse when he finally set eyes on Derrynane Abbey.

It was Sunday morning, and the sun was up, when Dan heard the knock on the door. Burke was summoned to the library after Dan was informed
of the horseman's trek from Cork. A dishevelled Burke presented his case in no uncertain terms: 'If you come they'll be safe; if not, they'll all be hanged.'

When he heard about the fate of the first four prisoners, Dan resolved to make it to Cork by Monday morning. That afternoon, he set out on his journey with a single horse and gig – a light carriage chosen for the long journey. The lonesome road taken had been described a month earlier by a German wanderer: 'Foreign travellers have probably never been thrown into this desolate corner of the earth, which belongs rather to owls

40

and sea-mews as to men, and of whose awful wildness it is difficult to give an idea.'

With lanterns blazing on his carriage, Dan made it to Macroom during the night of 25 October 1829. There he rested for three hours before again setting forth. The morning of 26 October sprang to life in Cork, and when the court sat for the second trial at 9 a.m. there was still no sign of Dan. Judge Robert Torrens refused an application to postpone until he arrived, but barely an hour into proceedings, with accompanying commotion and cheers, Dan entered the building.

He greeted the two judges. Richard Pennefather, an old colleague, welcomed him graciously. Torrens refused to acknowledge him. John Doherty went pale, and took a step back. The chief prosecutor now had a challenger. Dan flung off his frieze coat and apologised for his appearance – dirty and wet as he was. He requested breakfast, to which Pennefather agreed, and he was brought milk and sandwiches.

Dan scoffed the food. His table manners were said to have been bad, but that morning they were terrible. As Doherty was making a point to the jury, Dan shouted 'That's not law!' while his mouth was full of milk and bread. He slobbered more, and again interrupted with a jeer, 'That Act has expired!'

Doherty's stream of rumour and manufactured evidence was halted by the presence of Dan, the legal heavyweight. Right from the start he was proving to the judges and jury that the chief prosecutor was ignorant of the law. In a final insult, he mocked and mimicked Doherty's grand accent, much to the amusement of all present, and to the disgust of Doherty.

Dan finally stood and wiped the milk from his mouth. After cross-examining the 'approvers' (Whiteboys giving evidence against their brethren in return for freedom), Dan quickly established that they had been working together on their stories. He rounded on one of them, David Sheehan, as he began to find holes in his 'evidence'. Sheehan's constant use of the refined phrase 'I do not recollect' struck Dan as evidence in itself that he had been instructed on what to say. 'I never saw such well-drilled witnesses in my life,' Dan later barked to the jury.

As well as being coarse in the genteel company of the Ascendancy, Dan was aggressive in his questioning of the witnesses, and began shouting at them. Sheehan, under the spell of Dan's wrath, even admitted to making up the existence of another witness, a 'Mr Michael Nowlan'. Dan began to mock him, the evidence now in tatters. After a panicked attempt by Sheehan to justify himself, Dan exclaimed to the jury, 'This fellow is absolutely fatiguing me!'. Sheehan stepped down, disgraced and defeated.

As more 'approvers' came to the stand, they were similarly ensnared by Dan in a maze of confusion and contradiction. The entire trial was now unravelling. One approver even cried out in dejected misery, ''Tis little I thought I'd meet you here today, Councillor O'Connell.'

One juror exclaimed to the judges that he could 'not believe a tittle' of the witnesses' evidence. With the jury panel in disagreement, this second set of defendants was eventually discharged and freed.

In the third trial, Dan had the upper hand throughout, attacking the 'evidence' so thoroughly even Judge Pennefather backed him, calling the witnesses 'wretches' and 'monsters who have steeped their hands in repeated acts of blood'. It took the jury only minutes to find the latest batch of defendants not guilty.

The prosecution, under Doherty, decided not to proceed with charges against the remaining defendants because of 'the character of the evidence'. It was evidence that had been manipulated by themselves and dismantled by Dan.

On Friday 30 October 1829 the case was terminated, and the prisoners released. Dan had saved the lives of the accused, while the initial four death sentences were reduced to transportation. He had bullied the witnesses into a corner, and humiliated the corrupt prosecution. The result was achieved by combining his knowledge of the law with the force of his personality. Dan had performed his greatest triumph in a courthouse.

In the aftermath of the Doneraile trials, Dan condemned the Whiteboys, and assured them that their violence and bloodletting was not the key to freedom. He condemned the Crown, the prosecution and the commission that had been set up to annihilate peasant revolt, whatever the cost. He stood alone, seeking justice. He criticised anyone and everyone who did not act in a noble manner, no matter the class or creed. He was at the height of his powers.

Robert Peel, one of Dan's great enemies, would later pay him one of his biggest compliments. In company one evening, when asked his opinion on Dan's skills as a speaker, Peel replied: 'If I wanted an efficient and eloquent advocate, I would readily give up all the other orators of whom we have been talking, provided I had with me this broguing Irish fellow.'

DAN AND THE ACT OF UNION: 1800

'It is a curious thing enough that all the principles of my subsequent life are contained in my very first speech.'

Dan was here reflecting in old age with his friend William Joseph O'Neill Daunt.

The speech in question was a vehement dismissal of the proposed Act of Union, and was a significant moment in Dan's life. It was given on 13 January 1800, and its words could be seen as the definition of his cause, from that day forward, for the next forty-seven years.

Catholic Emancipation, the other great cause he championed, was always secondary; he saw it merely as a route to abolishing the Act of Union: 'I always said Repeal would be the consequence of Emancipation, and I always avowed such to be my object.'

The Rebellion two years previously had been the attempt by the United Irishmen to gain complete independence from Britain. But with its violent and bloody suppression, the outcome was the direct opposite of that aim. Prime Minister William Pitt now had all the reasons he needed to obliterate the Irish Parliament and transfer power directly to London. Within weeks of the start of the Rebellion he was putting in place plans to do just that, and by the end of 1798 the general terms of the union had been settled.

44

After a first attempt to pass the Act in 1799 had failed, the Government began to make a second, greater effort. It attempted to win votes by financial bribery and the promise of prestigious titles. It was outright corruption, which Dan later claimed was part of the Establishment's 'official *management*'. Most of these bribes were to indebted landlords whose vote could easily be swayed. Future favours were also promised to anyone who could help steer the Act through Parliament.

Pitt, along with the Chief Secretary in Dublin, Lord Castlereagh (Robert Stewart), and Lord Lieutenant Charles Cornwallis, tried to win the support of the Catholic hierarchy by promising Emancipation once the Act of Union had passed into law. One condition was made clear: so long as the Irish Parliament remained in existence, no such relief would be given to Catholics. This hierarchy – the bishops of the Catholic Church – was swayed by the Government's pledge and soon was on the side of the Establishment. Dan, however, considered the plans for union an act of treachery. He was at once determined to destroy the notion that the Church represented the voice of the people.

By this stage, he had been enjoying much success in the local courts, with his humour and contagious high spirits making him a popular figure in the Law Library, as well as the debating societies he had joined. These gatherings were trifles, however, and now Dan was planning his first speech of real significance. He didn't *write* a speech, in the traditional sense of penning a complete script. Instead, he made headings that he would elaborate on, in his own way. This was significant and would

45

establish the method he used to become a great orator, with a natural manner and aura, in the years to come.

Dan was determined to speak well at the Royal Exchange in Dublin, as the nature of oratory had been one of his great passions of study. 'While I apply myself to the English language,' he had told Hunting Cap in 1796, 'I endeavour to unite purity of diction to the harmony of phraseology.' Dan's lifelong ambition was to make it onto 'the great stage of the world' and he assured his uncle, 'I will endeavour to appear there with brilliancy.'

Four years later that stage was set. Ambrose Moore, an upstanding citizen, chaired the meeting. Dan sat in the wings, waiting apprehensively for his moment. But within minutes of the opening proceedings, panic set in when the sound of the Yeomanry marching down Parliament Street was heard. The sudden crash of muskets on flagstones outside awakened the large crowd of Catholic supporters to the imminent danger. Dan, with the help of a few others, calmed the crowd and advanced to meet the redcoats of the Yeomanry, and more specifically their commanding officer, Major Sirr.

Major Sirr demanded to see the resolutions up for debate. Fortunately, Dan had toned down the original, partisan notes written up by a senior lawyer, John Philpot Curran. When the Major was convinced there was no danger in the gathering, he threw the resolutions aside and reluctantly ordered his militia to retreat. And so, after this dramatic interruption, Ambrose called on Dan to step forward and speak.

Like many young people unaccustomed to addressing large numbers, Dan felt the pang of nervous excitement: 'My face glowed, and my ears tingled at the sound of my own voice, but I got more courage as I went on.' As nervous as he was, he settled into his speech, and was soon rousing the anti-Unionists present. It was, according to Robert Moore, a Drogheda native in the crowd, 'one of the best and most patriotic speeches that was ever uttered in any assembly'.

Dan assured his audience that a return to the Penal Laws 'in all its pristine horrors' would be a better alternative to laying down the country 'at the feet of foreigners'. A resounding cheer at the end elevated his first public speech to that of an emphatic triumph. Not only had he stepped into the arena of national politics, but he had done so on his terms, with the self-confidence to forge his own path, no matter who disagreed.

Hunting Cap, for one, was furious. *An Caipín*, as he was sometimes known, was a supporter of the Government. He had even been working on a campaign of support for the Union with another of Dan's uncles, John. Hunting Cap was also a close friend of Bishop Francis Moylan of Cork, who was a central figure in the Catholic hierarchy, which backed the Union.

Dan did not tell his uncle of his public appearance, but inevitably the press reports reached Derrynane. Hunting Cap's fury was tinged with embarrassment, given his connections and standing on the matter. Had he known about the meeting, or even suspected it, he would by no means have given permission for it. His reaction was immediate. Sensing that he was dealing with a naive young man, he assured Dan that 'popular applause is always short-lived, but the inconveniences may be serious and lasting'.

In the summer of 1800 two Acts of Union were passed, first in July at Westminster, and then in August in the Parliament of Ireland at College Green in Dublin. Together they made the United Kingdom of Great Britain and Ireland a reality.

Dan's usual summer escape to Kerry was marred by this stain on his nation. He journeyed from Killarney to Kenmare under a dark and mutinous sky. 'That desert district was congenial to impressions of solemnity and sadness,' he later remembered. 'Black giant clouds sailed slowly through the sky ... my soul felt dreary, and I had many wild and Ossianic inspirations as I traversed the bleak solitudes.'

New Year's Eve of 1800 was, in Dan's lifetime, the last moment when Ireland had the power to govern herself. True, it had been a power driven by the Ascendancy, but it was a form of self-rule nonetheless. Dan was in

Dublin the next day, Thursday 1 January 1801, and heard bells chiming out in celebration across the city 'as if it was a glorious national festival'.

Dan was convulsed with rage: 'My blood boiled.'

He vowed that day 'that the foul dishonour should not last, if *I* could ever put an end to it'.

MARY, EMANCIPATION AND REPEAL: 1800–10

While he was lamenting the loss of Ireland to the Union, Dan became distracted by a young woman. Mary O'Connell, his namesake, was the object of his affection. He was an impulsive young man, and within a few weeks of their acquaintance he asked her to marry him.

'I said to her, "Are you engaged, Miss O'Connell?"

'She answered, "I am not."

'"Then," said I, "will you engage yourself to me?"

'"I will," was her reply. And I said I would devote my life to make her happy.'

Much as Dan's speech against the Union was his first important step into public life, meeting Mary would be equally important for his personal happiness. She would provide Dan with stability and guidance for many years to come.

There was one big problem, though – Hunting Cap. Uncle Maurice had already made plans for Dan, in the form of Cork woman Miss Mary Anne Healy. Ms Healy was noted for her short stature and big nose. More importantly for Hunting Cap, she was also noted for having an even bigger purse – she was set to inherit a fortune. But Dan had his heart set on Mary O'Connell. Only weeks into their relationship he was confessing his love for her: 'I delight in repeating it that you are my first and only love ... I do declare to you by the God of Heaven that you are the only woman I have thus addressed as my intended wife.'

He was set to lose everything. Hunting Cap would disinherit him if he learnt of Dan's plans with the daughter of a lowly Tralee man. Dan was intent on keeping his new attachment secret, and begged Mary to visit him in Dublin. There they would be away from 'that prying, curious, *busy* town of Tralee'.

In the meantime, the pair had to make do with a top-secret correspondence. A number of friends and close relatives got involved in picking up, carrying and delivering the young couple's love letters.

As well as fearing Hunting Cap's reaction, Mary was worried about the potential gossip in the town. The Tralee postmaster's wife, Mrs Busteed,

was a well-known busybody and often took pleasure in reading private letters. Mary was already in delicate health with asthma, and prone to colds and coughs, and the stress of the situation did not help matters.

It was not until 24 July 1802, after twenty months of secret engagement, that they married – privately – in Dublin. The celebrations were not to last long, as Mary returned to Tralee only three days later, with Dan returning to the court circuit in Ennis shortly after.

With their marriage still a secret, they were not to meet again until September, when work took Dan to the Tralee assizes. While in town, Dan met Mary's grandmother, who knew nothing of the relationship. He made a point of insulting Mary to throw the old lady off the scent.

'Mary would do very well,' said Dan, 'only she is so cross.' Springing to her granddaughter's defence, the old lady replied: 'Sir, you must yourself be quite in fault. My little Mary was always the gentlest, sweetest creature born.'

Of course Dan knew it well, and two months later he was overjoyed when Mary announced she was pregnant with their first child. He wanted a girl, 'like her dear sweet mother, very fair and cherry cheeked with a saucy little nose'. While he was incredibly happy, he knew these new developments were sure to reach Hunting Cap's ear, sooner or later. It was time to bite the bullet.

The death of Dan's grandmother, Honora O'Mullane, over Christmas 1802, forced him to return to Derrynane. After the funeral, Dan skulked about the house for nine days, not knowing how he would break the news to his stern uncle. In the end he baulked, and instead wrote a letter, which his brother, John, was to give Hunting Cap at a convenient time.

Dan hoped for the best, but was soon brought down to earth when he learned his uncle reacted to the marriage and pregnancy by bursting into a most intense flood of tears. Hunting Cap was enraged, and sure enough he promptly disinherited his nephew. Dan's father, Morgan, was more understanding and quickly took to Mary, even inviting her to his house in Carhen.

Mary was no intellect, but she was a tough woman, and would bear ten children. In the first years of marriage she spent little time with Dan, but through it all, and for the duration of their time as husband and wife, they would address each other in the most affectionate terms. She was a staunch Catholic, and always practised her faith. She was the daughter of a mixed marriage, with her father and brothers being Protestants. Perhaps this made her more passionate about her religion, and she quickly brought Dan around to her way of thinking. He had half-heartedly practised Deism, but rejected it when Mary assured him of the power of prayer.

53

Such was the power of Dan's conversion that he wrote to Mary shortly after and told her he would spend every spare moment praying for her. Deism, he told her, was just 'a miserable philosophy, which I had taken up and been proud of. It now affords me no consolation.' It was said that had Mary not converted Dan, he would never have become the Catholic Liberator.

On 23 June 1803 their relationship deepened with the arrival of their first child, a boy they named Maurice. After the birth in Tralee, mother and child moved up to Dan's lodgings in Dublin.

Only a short month later, Dan returned from court in haste one afternoon and announced: 'I fear there is mischief in the wind.' The 'mischief' was a rebellion led by Robert Emmet, a Protestant and member of the United Irishmen. Dan was immediately summoned by messenger to take up his duties with the Lawyers' Corps.

The insurrection was badly managed and proved a complete failure for Emmet. The most notable casualty was the Lord Chief Justice, Viscount Kilwarden. Along with his nephew, Kilwarden was piked to death close to the gates of Dublin Castle. The fracas led Dan to dismiss Emmet in the aftermath:

At the head of eighty men, armed only with pikes, he waged war on the most powerful Government in the world, and the end of the mad fiasco was the murder of the best of the then Irish judges, Lord Kilwarden. He merits, and will suffer, the severest punishment. A man who could coolly prepare so much bloodshed, so many murders – and such horrors of every kind has ceased to be an object of compassion.

Fears of revolt were not confined to Dublin city, and in November Mary, back home, wrote to Dan happy with the news her husband would be joining a Yeomanry regiment in Kerry. The south-west of Ireland between 1802 and 1805 had seen a large outbreak of violence from Whiteboys. Night-time raids on houses by dozens of armed men had become the norm. In one case of intimidation in Tipperary, a woman was slain in order to drive her husband to quit his farm. Children were beaten and farmers' daughters were abducted. Mary hoped the Yeomanry would 'be able to keep down the common people. They are the only people I dread in this part of the world.'

Nor was Mary fond of the Irish spoken by many of the locals. Once, she informed Dan of a peasant girl who was entrusted to look after young Maurice. The girl was preferred 'to any other nurse, though she does not speak a word of English, which to me, you know, is unpleasant'. Compared to the vast majority of Irish Catholics, Dan and Mary were well educated, and worldly in their outlook. They viewed Irish as a barrier to self-improvement in a world dominated by English speakers. 'A diversity of tongues is no benefit,' Dan once told O'Neill Daunt. 'It would be of vast advantage to mankind if all the inhabitants of the earth spoke the same language.'

Dan believed Ireland and the Irish were being left behind, and he was determined to correct that. The Irish were a beaten-down race in the early nineteenth century, the people having no recollection of freedom, or a life without serious poverty. Random outbreaks of violence were quickly supressed by the Government, which then carried out the most barbaric

punishments. Hangings, gibbetings and beheadings were the sanctions of choice to keep the people in check.

According to Dan, you could tell a Catholic by 'his subdued and slavish look and gait'. He was determined to knock this servile attitude out of them. Each day he marched, rather than walked, to the Four Courts, chest thrust out and his umbrella carried over his shoulder like a pike. One magazine described these proud and defiant marches as Dan putting 'one factious foot in front of the other, as if he had already burst his bonds, and was kicking the Protestant Ascendancy before him'.

Unlike Dan, the Catholic leaders at the time were not men to fight the corner of their fellow countrymen.

'When I took the helm,' reflected Dan, 'I found all Catholics full of mutual jealousies – one man trying to outrival another – one meeting rivalling another – the leaders watching to sell themselves to the highest penny!'

It was with these old connivers and plotters that Dan made his first venture into formal politics, in November 1804. The Catholic Committee, previously called the Catholic Board, was under the leadership of noblemen and landed proprietors. This Catholic Board had been far from radical, and most obedient to the Crown.

Dan pushed himself forward within the new Catholic Committee. He was determined to make his mark, and straightaway he was promoted to a small subcommittee entrusted with writing up a petition for the complete abolition of the Penal Laws. The petition was to be presented at Parliament in London the following spring.

Dan was now working all hours, and was without an idle moment. Although he was up before eight every morning, he could not get through half his business. He was mixing family life – a second son, Morgan, had just been born – with his professional life. Add to this his new and determined adventure with the Catholic Committee and it is hardly surprising that his days were so full.

'The fate of millions perhaps depends on my poor pen,' he told Mary in December 1804. 'There are five appointed for *this* purpose. We must have the petition ready for Sunday. Until then believe me that I shall sleep little.'

However busy he was, Dan assured Mary that his role as the family breadwinner was not being disrupted: 'Heart, my *law* business goes on right well.'

But in truth Dan was willing to sacrifice himself to the detriment of his finances by volunteering to go with the petition to London the following March. He stood to lose one quarter of a year's earnings by taking time off from his legal work. In the end, his junior status at the committee prevented him from travelling.

As it was, the plight of Irish Catholics was of little concern to the Establishment at this time. Napoleon's French armies had been triumphing across Europe, with decisive victories at Genoa, Ulm and later Austerlitz. The British monarchy of King George III was in absolute fear of invasion. William Pitt's qualities as a leader had helped him regain the job of Prime Minister. His appointment was an attempt by the King to

(L-r): Daniel O'Connell, King George III and Napoleon Bonaparte

prevent a war on his own shores. As Pitt had backed Catholic Emancipation only five years before, the travelling delegation from Dublin felt he would help their cause and support their petition. They were wrong. Pitt had promised the King he would never again raise the Catholic question, fearing another bout of the 'madness' – or dementia – that had been plaguing the monarch.

Dejected, the travelling committee members turned to Charles James Fox, a Whig politician, who argued their case in the House of Commons. His argument was rejected by the majority of MPs. The defeat of the petition was a cause of despair for the Catholic leadership, but it confirmed how right Dan had been. As Ireland was now legally tied to Great Britain, the rights of Irish Catholics were of little importance to the Tory Government. Dan saw that the Catholic hierarchy had been sold a lie by Pitt on the eve of the Union. Emancipation be damned, the Union was sealed. The Catholic case for support of that Union had now been swept away.

Dan still lacked the age and experience to be the senior voice of the committee, however. With the death of Pitt in early 1806, the Catholic old order was given some hope when its apparent supporter, Charles James Fox, joined the new Government – the so-called Ministry of All the Talents. Fox assured Irish Catholics he would raise the question of their rights, but must be allowed time to deal with the Napoleonic Wars raging on the Continent. Yet Fox, for all his promises, never spoke up for the Catholics, fell ill in July and died two months later.

Dan grew impatient with the old order in the committee. He would not sit back, and instead argued his point with the leadership. They believed constant petitions to Parliament for a hopeless cause was ridiculous. Dan believed the cause was worth pursuing. He lived in a country that was overwhelmingly Catholic in tradition and population. He sought justice for that population, and would not rest.

His legal career had by now flourished into an immense success. He was commanding huge fees. Senior barristers were often ignored to let

Dan, a junior, take a case. Yet he could not climb the ladder of his profession because he was a Catholic. It did not matter that he was a better man of law than all around him, and most above him – men he looked upon as his inferiors.

That a Catholic could not stand in Parliament to argue for his rights vexed Dan still further. He felt there was only one thing to do: continue to agitate and petition.

When the case for a new petition on abolishing the Penal Laws came up at a meeting in January 1808, the Catholic Committee's Mr O'Connor and Mr Clinch wanted it postponed. They argued that another campaign would only expose them to 'the mockery and insult of men in power; to division, rejection and defeat'.

Dan rose to speak, and he did so now with the power and range that had seen his law career prosper. He threw aside all courtesy; the day for that was gone. His voice boomed across the room. He labelled the MPs Perceval, Canning, Jenkinson and Castlereagh as upstarts who were 'pompous, petulant, inane'. In a personal insult, Dan said Canning was nothing more than a bad poet. He spoke as a man looking not just for his own liberty, but for that of the generations to follow.

'If it was the liberty of their children the present petition sought, would O'Connor and Clinch postpone it for an hour?'

He won the argument, and the proposal to petition was carried through. As expected, when Henry Grattan presented it at Westminster, it was rejected by a large majority. Again, a year later, the same result. But by agitating, forcing the issue and refusing to give in, Dan was emerging as the new leader of the Catholic Committee. By 1810 he was ready to tackle another matter that had been in preparation for years: to repeal, or abolish, the Act of Union. Dan was part of a nine-man team that drew up a petition to the King in favour of Repeal.

Dublin in 1810 had seen the ruin of trade and business over the previous decade, a consequence of the loss of an Irish Parliament. The merchants of the city, although largely Protestant, were in no doubt that to halt Dublin's decline the Union between Ireland and Britain needed to be severed. At a meeting in September, Dan stood before a congregation of businessmen, made up of Protestants and Orangemen, as well as a scattering of Catholics. He denounced the Union: 'The Union was a manifest injustice, and it continues to be unjust to this day; it was a crime, and must be still criminal, unless it shall be pretended that crime, like wine, improves by old age. England stole upon us like a thief in the night and robbed us of the precious gem of our liberty.'

It was now, in 1810, that Dan reinforced his view that Repeal – bursting the bonds with London – was the priority. The petition written for the King included details of Ireland's debts, as well as the money that was leaving the country in the form of rents to absentee landlords. The state of danger and distress in rural Ireland was also discussed.

'We have resigned our independence to a foreign legislature, in a foreign country,' Dan said. 'The object was not to unite us, but to reduce us to the situation of servitude.'

The harsh and critical speech on the Union was hailed as a great success. Dan had emerged as the leader of the Catholic cause. His new fame saw his image appear on the cover of *Dublin Magazine*. The portrait was captioned 'Councillor O'Connell'.

'Enquire the first day you go to town about it,' he proudly told Mary. When she bought a copy she teased Dan about looking like a little prince.

Henry Grattan then invited him to a dinner party. It was Dan's formal entry to the top tier of Irish society. He boasted about it later: 'I was then beginning to be talked of, and people like to see a young person who acquires notoriety.'

Grattan had entered Parliament as an MP for the Patriot Party in 1775, the year of Dan's birth, and had long been a hero to the new 'Councillor'. But by the end of 1810 Dan was forging his own path. He would later be asked who he thought was the greatest Irishman. 'Harry Grattan,' was the reply. 'Next to myself.'

Enemy of the State: 1810–15

Only two months had passed since Dan's great speech against the Union when George III was suddenly removed from his throne. It was well known the King suffered with dementia. Now, in November 1810, the death of his sickly daughter Amelia proved too much for his sanity.

The House of Commons introduced a regency bill, which meant the King's son George, Prince of Wales, would now carry out his father's duties. As the Prince of Wales had been an old friend of a previous supporter of the Catholic cause, Charles James Fox, the Catholic Committee in Dublin thought the new Prince Regent might prove a welcome change. However, he showed little interest in the Catholic question, and Dan would later remark that 'there never was a greater scoundrel than that prince'.

Throughout 1811 repeated attempts were made to suppress the Catholic Committee and to jail its leaders. Dan welcomed the prospect, for it would bring attention to their cause or, as he put it, 'keep the business alive'. As well as suppressing the Catholic hierarchy, the Government continued to carry out the severest punishments on common Catholics throughout the country. For instance, in early 1811, seven men had been hanged in front of thousands at Ballyduff, County Tipperary. Their crime had been an assault on a prosperous farmer. It was in this environment of social unrest that Dan cranked up his agitation for Catholic rights.

Dan realised the obedient route taken by the older Catholic leaders was no use, and he began to use violent language against the Crown. It was reported in July that Dan had claimed Catholic rights could be gained only by use of violence, with weapons. Given his hatred of armed struggle it is possible these words were used merely to whip up excitement for the cause. At a meeting that month, Dan strongly urged that the Catholic Committee be expanded, both in numbers and geographically. The decision to add ten Catholics from each county, and five from each Dublin parish, forced the Government to intervene.

Using the Convention Act of 1793, Spencer Perceval, the Prime Minister, wasted no time in declaring illegal the appointment of county or parish representatives to the Committee. Shortly after, a number of people were brought before the courts on charges of organising the elections of these county and parish members. For one of these trials, that of Edward Sheridan, Dan was unable to act for the defence, but he designed it so well that the King's prosecutors were left embarrassed when the jury found the defendant not guilty.

It was a small victory for Dan and the Committee. The Establishment, however, influenced by the Prince Regent, was determined to bring the Catholic movement to a halt. On 23 December 1811, Committee members gathered again, but a police magistrate was already at the hall. The Committee members initially refused to leave and demanded a legal explanation. Then, led by Dan, they moved to a private house. The magistrate followed, so they again moved off – this time to a pub in Dublin's inner city. It was a farcical situation, but it showed the determination of the Government to keep the voice of the Catholics down.

The constant harassment forced Dan to break up the Committee, and instead start a new Catholic Board from scratch. The Government at Dublin Castle persisted with its legal persecution, and continued to charge those who had organised county and parish elections. Dan turned the behaviour of the Government to his advantage, however. On his court circuit of spring 1812 he stood before meetings of Munster Catholics and admonished the system, shouting down the arrogant behaviour of the Prince Regent's forces, as well as condemning the Act of Union, 'that grave of Irish prosperity'.

In May 1812, the heart of the British Establishment was struck a deadly blow. While Prime Minister Perceval was walking through the lobby of the House of Commons, a man stepped forward, drew a pistol and shot

him in the chest. The assassin, John Bellingham, acted alone and out of a grievance of being unjustly imprisoned. While the murder was met with shock and grief in London, there was hope in Dublin that a Government under a new leader would be kinder to the Catholic cause.

There was to be no such luck. Only a month previously, the Prince Regent had, in haughty and contemptuous terms, refused to meet travelling members of the Catholic Board. He also strongly supported a new anti-Catholic regime under Lord Liverpool, Robert Jenkinson.

At a Catholic meeting on Fishamble Street in Dublin, Dan poured scorn on the Prince Regent. In a highly controversial move, he attacked the Prince Regent's mistress, Lady Hertford, for her 'witchery'. He accused her of being 'an unworthy secret influence' on the monarch-in-waiting. Then, much to the shock and ire of the more timid members of the Catholic Board, Dan insulted the not-long-dead Perceval: 'For my part I feel unaffected horror at his fate, but I do not forget that he was a narrow-minded bigot, a paltry statesman, and a bad Minister.'

Dan called Perceval a supporter of 'every species of public corruption'. The late Prime Minister, said Dan, was an enemy of reform and an enemy of liberty. These words were nothing short of treason in the eyes of Dublin Castle and London. He was quickly becoming an enemy of the State, not for turning, and the true defender of the Irish people:

'We are strong in the justice of our cause and in the inextinguishable right of man, in every soil and climate, to unlimited liberty of conscience. Let us, however, expect nothing from the courts and ministers.'

Dan quoted the English poet Lord Byron, asserting to his fellow Irish Catholics that it must be themselves who rose up. They must not stand by passively and wait for a foreign foe to emancipate them:

Hereditary bondsmen! know ye not
Who would be free themselves must strike the blow?

Needless to say, this kind of agitation was not welcomed by the Government, not least as it was a time of national crisis for Britain. Europe was increasingly coming under the rule of the French Empire, with Napoleon Bonaparte's *Grande Armée* recording success after success on the Continent. Just a week after Dan's speech at Fishamble Street the French troops crossed the Neman River in a big push east to conquer Russia. If Napoleon succeeded there, an invasion of England and Ireland would quickly follow. 'Let us be only masters of the English Channel for six hours, and we shall be masters of the world,' Bonaparte had declared.

Knowing a strong ministry was vital in a time of such crisis, future Prime Minister George Canning sought to address the Catholic question, which had split the Government. His summer proposal to tackle Catholic rights in the next session of Parliament was supported by a large majority in the House of Commons.

Unlike most of the Catholic Board, Dan reacted to the proposal with strong hostility. He knew any relief the Government would give to Irish Catholics would be coupled with 'religious securities', or the 'veto' as it would come to be known. This 'veto' was a clause that would allow the Protestant monarchy to retain control over the Catholic Church. Dan called on all Irish Catholics to demand total Emancipation, free from any clauses or 'securities' that were there simply to calm Protestant fears of liberated Catholics.

At this stage, fourteen years on from his entrance to the legal profession, Dan began to resent the stifling effects of the Penal Laws. Forced to remain a junior barrister, he had to take to the Munster circuit again in the autumn of 1812, continuing to take small cases for minimal fees. 'I have as yet *my* full share of it,' he wrote to Mary. 'I hate this kind of business excessively. Darling, you ought to hope for Emancipation that I may get rid of the annoyance of it.'

Busy and weary as he was, Dan sought out the mountains for peace of mind and a spot of hunting. After the September courts in Tralee, he and his friend James Butler got lost in the Kerry Mountains chasing red grouse. He was in upbeat mood after it.

'I had a delightful day of it,' said Dan. 'What pleased me very much was to find that I was as well able to trot the mountains as ever I was.'

Rural Ireland was experiencing a prosperous economic spell. The war in Europe had boosted the demand for Irish farming products, and the autumn of 1813 in particular saw the return of a good harvest.

'The rents are coming in extremely fast without the smallest trouble,' wrote Dan. 'The poor people have a most abundant year of it.'

Yet, even if a peasant's 'abundance' was simply an ability to pay his rent, it was not to last, as a sudden and extended slump in prices arrived in the following years.

And so the question of Catholic conditions and rights rumbled on. The restrictions put upon them, and the system they were bound to, kept the majority of Irish people in a state of slavery. Full rights for all was Dan's demand. When a relief bill that included clauses and securities failed in 1813, he was far from upset.

Dan had strongly criticised Henry Grattan for supporting the flimsy bill. In Dan's mind, to accept a Protestant monarch's power over the Catholic Church was to abandon the identity of his people. In agreeing to the veto, he said, Grattan had given up 'our honour and our religion'.

In the same public address, Dan insisted the bill, with its continued subservience to the Crown and corrupt Protestant leaders, was the work of the Lord Lieutenant Charles Lennox and his Chief Secretary, Robert Peel.

The recently appointed Peel was, claimed Dan, only 'a raw youth ... sent over here before he got rid of the foppery of perfumed handkerchiefs and thin shoes'. For these most public insults Dan received great praise, not least for coining the nickname 'Orange Peel'.

Not surprisingly, after these initial personal attacks, the two men would go on to be lifelong foes.

67

Lennox, otherwise known as the Duke of Richmond, was likewise offended. His distinguishing characteristic as chief governor was, according to Dan, 'that he continues bitterly to hate the papists – he knows not why'. Shortly after, when the Duke retired, the *Dublin Evening Post* newspaper printed a series of articles that criticised the administration of the country under him. Peel wanted to put down the pro-Catholic newspapers, and on 26 July a case of libel was brought against John Magee – the owner, printer and publisher of the *Dublin Evening Post*. Dan defended Magee, in a case that became more about politics and English rule in Ireland than about Magee's defence. It was to become one of Dan's great triumphs as an agitator.

To Magee's horror, Dan had decided the case was lost for his client from the start. Dan decided to use the time in court to widely and roundly criticise the Government, all but abandoning Magee to his fate.

At the beginning of the trial, William Saurin, the Attorney General, delivered a stinging tirade against Magee. Among other things, he called the accused a 'ruffian', a 'revolutionary' and 'abominable'. Dan wasted no time in belittling Saurin, calling his arguments 'a confused and disjointed tissue of bigotry and vulgarity'.

Daniel O'Connell, a junior barrister, was thrashing the chief law enforcer in Ireland in full view of the Establishment. Robert Peel himself was among a crowd of Protestants stunned by the onslaught. Peel would later say that if Magee was guilty of publishing a libel, Dan's words at the court case were a whole lot worse.

As Dan continued to insult Saurin he left the Attorney General livid and open-mouthed in amazement. Beads of sweat trickled down his forehead and his lips were white. So sorry for him were the crowd that even Peel felt obliged to console him with kind whispers.

In defence of Magee, Dan argued that the printed articles about the Duke's administration could not be libellous because, in fact, they were true. The articles had described previous Lord Lieutenants – Westmorland, Camden and Cornwallis – as unprincipled, cruel and treacherous. Dan said these descriptions were indeed correct.

He used the 'cruel' Camden administration to illustrate his point: 'On one circuit during Camden's administration there were one hundred individuals tried before one judge; of these ninety-eight were capitally convicted, and ninety-seven hanged! I understand one escaped; but he was a soldier who murdered a peasant, or something of that *trivial* nature. *Ninety-seven* victims in one circuit!'

Of the Duke of Richmond himself, Dan supported the *Dublin Evening Post*'s claims that the Lord Lieutenant had begun his job 'ignorant' of Ireland and Irish Government policy. In a cunning aside, Dan took a sympathetic tack, allowing that, as a military man abroad, Richmond 'could not have any urge to make himself acquainted with the details of our barbarous wrongs, of our senseless party quarrels, and criminal feuds'.

So, the *Dublin Evening Post* had been accurate, and not at all libellous. Using the examples of both Richmond's 'ignorant' administration and previous Governments, Dan went on to denounce British mismanagement of Ireland over the previous twenty-five years. He was now acting as a political agitator, not a defence lawyer, and the whole room, packed with the Protestant Establishment, sat aghast at the audacity of this junior counsel.

He was not intimidated by the elite crowd. He stated boldly that when discussing public subjects and the administration of public men, 'truth is *a duty*, and not *a crime*'. With these words – the tenets of the freedom of speech and of the rights of man – Dan was defending himself, and Magee. His anti-Government address did little to help his client, however. The jury, packed with ultra-Protestant sympathisers, found Magee guilty with little hesitation.

69

Although Dan had seen his client condemned to the prison cell, he had won something important. For the first time he had confronted his enemies head on. His speech had lasted an epic four and a half hours. His opponents – the judge and his jury, Chief Secretary Peel, Attorney General Saurin and others from Dublin Castle – had been forced by the rules of court to sit there and listen to every dismissive word.

To make matters worse for Peel and his cohorts, the speech would be published widely in both England and Ireland. Magee's *Dublin Evening Post* immediately printed it, word for word. Pamphlets were issued throughout Ireland, read by the thousand. It was translated into French and Spanish. The speech and its reception marked a new high for Dan as a champion of the Irish Catholics.

Saurin was still reeling. The following November he initiated another case to increase Magee's sentence for publishing Dan's speech at the first trial. At this second trial, the Attorney General declared that Dan's July performance had been 'such an outrage on public decency as has not occurred in the memory of man'. Saurin went on to accuse Dan of participating in Magee's criminality.

Dan stunned the judges with his reply. He said the courtroom afforded the Attorney General a cowardly protection; otherwise he would receive the 'chastisement' he deserved. Chastisement was another word for horsewhipping, or a beating. The judges were aghast, and demanded a retraction. Dan stood his ground, until finally Saurin retracted his own false accusations. With that minor victory, Dan went on to say that Saurin was 'some creature, narrow-minded, mean, of inveterate bigotry'.

70

Magee quickly lost patience with Dan. His tactic of continuing to insult the prosecution was merely digging a deeper hole for his client, and Magee wanted him off the case. It was soon announced that Dan was dismissed and another lawyer appointed. Dan defended his actions, gaining what he could from a trial that was never going to be fair.

Whatever the outcome of the Magee trials, Dan's increasing fame led to huge rewards in his professional life. In Limerick, for instance, of twenty-six cases heard at the 1813 autumn assizes, Dan was involved in every one. His stock in the political world since the trials was low, however, so much so that in December the Catholic Board held a public display to demonstrate that Dan still had the backing of the Irish people. It was decided to present Dan with a silver plate, worth 1,000 guineas. The Board's John Finlay made a speech heaping praise on Dan, 'the agitator': 'History will describe Daniel O'Connell spotless in the relations of private life, matchless in the duties of private friendship, beloved by every man who knows him, esteemed by all who have not a prejudice or an interest in disliking him.'

Since the fallout of the Magee trials, the *Dublin Evening Post* had withdrawn its support for the Catholic Board. This left Dan and the Board without a public voice, as its meetings and discussions would not be published. Peel hoped this would cause the Board and its chief 'agitator' simply to fade away. When this did not occur, Peel sought to silence them by using the Convention Act of 1793, which had banned 'unlawful assemblies'. He got his way, and in June a proclamation was issued, declaring the Catholic Board an illegal body. Despite being controversial, the proclamation was accepted, and by the end of June the Board was dissolved.

Yet the fight for Emancipation went on, with informal and public meetings taking place. But it was now all the more difficult a battle. Even before the Government had intervened, the Catholic cause had been running aground.

The support the Catholics had hoped and failed to get from the Prince

Regent was one thing. By early 1813 the changing international situation diminished the cause even further. In the middle of a hard-fought foreign war many Members of Parliament believed peace in Ireland was absolutely necessary. But Napoleon's winter campaign in Russia had been a disaster, and now he was beginning to lose ground fast to Britain and her allies. With his defeat looming, and Britain on the cusp of victory, London was now far from concerned about the fate of Ireland's Catholics.

On top of all this, Dan's refusal to compromise on the veto was obstructing the chances of any form of Emancipation. His position was being challenged from all sides. A division had emerged in the Catholic Board ever since Dan's criticism of Grattan's support of the veto in 1813. In the spring of 1814, the Vatican also got involved. In place of Pope Pius VII – who had been taken prisoner by the French in 1809 – Monsignor Quarantotti wrote from Rome. He supported the British Government on its proposed clauses to full Catholic Emancipation.

Dan was infuriated by the interference of the Monsignor on such a political matter, and believed the Vatican had no right to get involved. He was adamant that if any of the Catholic clergy accepted the veto, the Irish people would turn against them:

'If the present clergy shall descend from the high station they hold, to become the vile slaves of Dublin Castle, the people will despise them too much.'

In fact, many of the Church hierarchy on the Catholic Board had stepped down before its suppression in that summer of 1814, believing Dan's fight was irrational and hopeless.

However, Dan was already the champion of the people, and the Irish clergy would soon back him unconditionally. Even with Rome

Vatican seal

72

declaring support for the veto, with many of the Board having walked out, and with the Government more than ever ignoring the Catholic question, Dan was unyielding in his cause.

On the veto issue, in January 1815, he addressed the congregation from the altar of Clarendon Street Church:

'I am sincerely a Catholic but *I am not Papist*,' he declared. 'Let our determination never to consent reach Rome ... should it fail I am still determined to resist.'

From the pulpit, in the midst of defending the rights of his people, Dan abused the Protestant Dublin Corporation by labelling it 'the beggarly Corporation'. Though the words may have seemed harmless at the time, their utterance would foreshadow yet another defining moment in his life.

DAN AND A TALE OF THREE DUELS: 1813–15

On many occasions, Dan's reputation and good name had been publicly assaulted. His honour as a man had been tested. Of course, he too had challenged the honour of others, with his damning put-downs and public ridicule. He had crossed the line when he struck John Segerson with a cane, and had been fortunate to escape the incident without a duel.

But on 13 August 1813, Dan finally stepped onto the field of battle, pistol in hand. The sails of a towering mill turned slowly behind Limerick's

Windmill Fields as Dan stood before the man he had challenged – his 'friend' Maurice Magrath.

The previous day in court Dan had insulted Magrath, who was the opposing counsel, by shouting 'That's a lie, Maurice!' Magrath responded by throwing a legal book at Dan's head, before kicking his shins under the table. Dan retaliated by striking Magrath in the face.

Dan then stormed out and went to another friend, Nicholas Purcell O'Gorman, and told him what had happened. Still furious at Magrath, Dan insisted on a challenge and asked O'Gorman to act as his second. O'Gorman tried to dissuade Dan from such a dramatic – even lethal – course of action, pointing out that he had already carried out the 'required' retaliation: a public strike, as opposed to O'Gorman's kick, which nobody saw.

But nothing would calm Dan and the duel was promptly organised. The next morning, at dawn, the two squabbling friends arrived on the field, together with their entourages of prominent merchants and squireens. While O'Gorman was pacing the field, taking measurements, a mutual friend of the combatants, N. P. Leader, approached Dan. Leader told Dan he was about to fight a man with whom he had no quarrel.

As the parties began to near a peace agreement, O'Gorman returned from the field and was furious to discover that, as Dan's second, he had not been consulted. Dan agreed to do whatever O'Gorman decided, but as O'Gorman placed a box of pistols in his hands the assembled crowd kicked up an almighty fuss. There would be blood on O'Gorman's hands, they insisted, and he should be hanged if one man fell to his death that morning. O'Gorman became agitated and upset, and told Dan he was resigning as his second.

Leader's compromise was agreed upon and not a shot was fired. The decision to quit the battlefield may have saved Dan's life, but it also raised questions about his courage. Some said he was a coward. His brother-in-law, Rickard, said Dan's decision to abort the duel left him with an 'unfavourable impression' that created 'serious uneasiness'.

75

The accusation of cowardice hung over Dan for two years. Even the goading and insults he had thrown at William Saurin during the Magee trials were seen as playing it safe – Saurin was simply written off as the greater coward of the two.

It was a Dublin merchant, John Norcott D'Esterre, who threw down the gauntlet that finally gave Dan the chance to prove his mettle. Ten days before their duel on 1 February 1815, Dan had made the infamous quip about the 'beggarly' Dublin Corporation. The Corporation had been petitioning against Catholic Emancipation. Ironically, D'Esterre was one of the few Protestants in the Corporation who was pro-Emancipation, but he had taken exception to the term 'beggarly'. He was going through money problems and took the insult personally.

D'Esterre was a deadly marksman – lethal with a gun. His bravery, too, was legendary. During the Nore mutiny of 1797 – when English sailors had protested about work conditions – he was held aloft in the rigging of a ship called the *Sandwich*. With a noose around his neck and bound hand and foot, he was given the chance to speak, to join the mutineers and save his life. Instead he hurled a defiant cry: 'No. Never! Hang away and be damned. God save the King!' So impressed were his captors, they hauled him down and he later escaped.

If Dublin Castle wanted to silence Dan, it could not have wished for a better man to carry out the task. The reasons for the duel may have been personal, but D'Esterre was also an Establishment man. Dan's attacks on William Saurin had not been forgotten, and Saurin's son was now a supporter of D'Esterre. So too was Abraham Bradley King, a former and future Dublin Lord Mayor. If Dan did not fight, his honour and personal reputation would be ruined. If he did, he faced certain death. Or so it was thought.

A series of to-and-fro correspondence led to Dublin being a frenzy of excitement and rumour. The streets were turned to pure theatre. 'Was there ever such a scene?' Dan would later wonder. D'Esterre gloried in the spotlight. He boasted to a large assembly of the Corporation that he would either flog Dan on the street or shoot him.

It looked as if a flogging was in store when D'Esterre arrived at the Four Courts on Tuesday 31 January 1815 brandishing a horsewhip. Dan was working inside, but when he arrived outside his challenger had fled. Further offended by this petty behaviour, Dan sent a deputy with a message to D'Esterre, declaring he would fight 'in three minutes whenever he chose'. D'Esterre threw back the message, insisting the challenge should come from Dan himself.

Dan tired of the prolonged drama. After trying and failing to catch D'Esterre on the streets, he decided silence was the best course of action. With nothing happening, Sir Edward Stanley, D'Esterre's second, finally lost patience and on the morning of 1 February set out to confront both Dan and his second – Major William Nugent McNamara. Both refused to speak on the matter. This caused an irritated Stanley, finally and formally, to issue the challenge. 'Very well,' responded McNamara, before insisting on the duel going ahead within three hours.

As McNamara had accepted the challenge it was within his rights to name the time and place. Stanley was taken aback by the speed with

which events had moved along. He pushed to postpone the contest until the next day, but failed to persuade McNamara. They finally agreed upon a 3.30 p.m. confrontation, set for Bishop's Court in Kildare, some 13 miles outside Dublin.

Dan and his entourage arrived half an hour early. They were welcomed by a large gathering that had congregated on a hill overlooking the battleground. In attendance too, but hidden away in a cabin, was a priest, Fr O'Mullane. He was going against the Church's wishes by being anywhere near a duel, but he was another radical, and felt a moral obligation to be on hand to give Dan the last rites, should that be called for.

Although most of Dublin Corporation was in attendance, Dan's support was far greater. There was a fear that if he were shot a riot would ensue. D'Esterre's support was ready for just such an event: Richard O'Gorman (Nicholas Purcell O'Gorman's brother) counted up to thirty-six pistols in enemy hands.

There was such menace in the air that Stanley believed it now highly dangerous for the duel to go ahead. He called for a postponement, but backtracked when he was assured that, as he was the one who issued the challenge, anything less than a duel would now be seen as cowardice. In an attempt to calm the atmosphere, D'Esterre made a speech that praised the Catholics. He assured the animated throng his quarrel with Dan had nothing to do with religion.

Dan took a moment to speak with his friend Charles Philips. Dan surprised the young lawyer by saying he had prepared for this day. Being such a public man, he assured Philips, he had thought of it as his duty to prepare, for his own protection, against such unprovoked aggression.

Dan had been given two pistols by his friend Richard Newton Bennett, who was now busy loading them. Stanley had no experience with firearms and called on a friend, Frederick Piers, to load D'Esterre's guns. The skies darkened and a light snow began to fall.

A call went up and the crowd suddenly went silent. Fr O'Mullane sat in prayer. Dan stood with pistols drawn at his sides. When the moment of truth arrived, D'Esterre raised his weapons and theatrically crossed them on his chest. He was too quick for Dan and got off the first shot. However, the bullet dipped short of its target and hit the turf. Immediately Dan raised his gun, aimed low, and fired. D'Esterre staggered. He turned a little on his right leg, then stumbled and fell flat on his face.

'Huzza for O'Connell!' came the cheer from the crowd. Blood began to stain the snow, and doctors surrounded the stricken D'Esterre.

Dan quietly made his way from the ground. It was not a moment he could – or ever would – celebrate.

Dan and his brother made their way back to Dublin, sitting in solemn silence as their carriage trundled into the city. Night had fallen, with the oil lamps dimly burning, when Dan finally spoke: 'I fear he is dead, he fell so suddenly.' His brother suggested he had struck D'Esterre about the head. 'That cannot be,' said Dan. 'I aimed low. The ball must have entered near the thigh.'

In fact, the shot had entered D'Esterre in the lower abdomen, and he was not to recover. Within two days he would be dead. Fearing a reaction from Dublin Castle, Dan immediately went into hiding at the home of a friend, Denys Scully. He quickly employed his brother to seek out his close colleague, the barrister Richard Pennefather, to defend him in case of his arrest. The city outside Scully's house was abuzz with excitement, and several bonfires were ablaze on street corners. Seven hundred merchants marched to Dan's house on Merrion Square to show their support. On learning he was absent, they all left their personal cards in a show of solidarity. One archbishop, on hearing of Dan's victory – despite the Church's opposition to duelling – even exclaimed, 'Heaven be praised! Ireland is safe!'

All of Dan's fears were laid to rest a few days later. 'There is not the most distant intention of any prosecution on the part of the family or friends of the late Mr D'Esterre,' wrote Edward Stanley, in a letter to Dan. Indeed, while on his deathbed, D'Esterre had let it be known that it was he who provoked Dan, and should bear the responsibility for the outcome.

Dan was relieved by Stanley's letter, and replied instantly:

Believe me, my regret at that event is most sincere and unaffected ... no person can feel for the loss society has sustained in the death of Mr D'Esterre with more deep and lasting sorrow than I do.

Dan's sorrow was genuine and he was determined to help the widow and two small children D'Esterre had left behind. The widow, Annie, refused the offer to share Dan's income, but accepted a yearly financial allowance given to the youngest child.

The duel and its outcome haunted Dan for the rest of his life. He would forever after tip his hat, lower his head and mutter a prayer when passing D'Esterre's house on Bachelor's Walk.

Whatever his thoughts were in the immediate aftermath, Dan wasted no time in getting back to his professional duties.

Only days after the duel he turned his mind to resurrecting the Catholic cause. At an aggregate meeting it was resolved to send a new petition for Catholic Emancipation to the House of Commons. But Henry Grattan refused to present it, and this heralded the final split in the Catholic camp.

It was agreed that Sir Henry Parnell (great-uncle of Charles Stewart) would go to Westminster instead. He argued the case for full Emancipation on 18 May 1815 but, predictably, when the vote came twelve days later the motion was defeated by a large majority.

On the same day, Chief Secretary Robert Peel stood in the House of Commons and criticised Dan. Referring to an anti-English speech he had made, Peel said the words used had made any goodwill an 'impossibility'. Dan responded with a highly inflammatory speech in which he suggested the Chief Secretary would never insult him were they face-to-face.

The accusation of cowardice was taken to Peel by a police reporter and forced him to act. He sent a friend in Ireland, Charles Saxton, to find Dan and sort out the matter, whatever course of action was required. After Saxton confronted Dan and nothing had been resolved, a duel seemed inevitable. Dan employed a friend, George Lidwell, to act on his behalf. On Friday 1 September 1815, Lidwell told Dan to have horses ready to bring him to a field in Kildare, where a duel to the death was now likely to take place.

At the final meeting of the two seconds, there seemed to have been an argument and some confusion about what exactly the duel was over and who should be the one to issue the challenge. In the heat of the moment, Saxton and Lidwell fell out. The following day Saxton published a highly offensive letter in the *Correspondent* newspaper criticising both Dan and Lidwell for their conduct. Lidwell was furious and immediately issued Saxton with a challenge of his own. This pair eventually met on a battleground in France. Maybe time had healed their grievances, for they both conveniently missed their targets.

Dan was angered by the way the affair had seemingly ended and wrote a scathing public letter of his own. He accused Peel of playing 'a paltry trick' and also of cowardice, preferring 'a paper war' to the real thing. In response, Peel wrote a letter directly to Dan, advising him to get a new second, or 'friend', who would get the wheels in motion for the duel finally to take place. That night Dan wrote to the Knight of Kerry, Maurice Fitzgerald: 'I want a friend most sadly and venture to think of you.' The Knight agreed to assist in the grisly affair.

Dan was determined to keep the duel a secret from his wife. He was running up massive debts. Not only could Mary be left a widow (now with six children under the age of twelve), but in all probability a penniless one at that. He was never good with money, but during these times he squandered thousands of pounds. He made loans to people far too eagerly, and was close to financial ruin.

In all probability, Mary had heard about the quarrel with Peel from reading the fighting words in the newspapers. She decided to act, and informed the sheriff of her husband's intentions. Early the next morning Dan stepped onto the landing from his room and was swiftly apprehended by two officers who had entered the house. They placed him under house arrest.

This was an almighty embarrassment. The Count, Daniel Charles O'Connell, was on a holiday in Ireland and was staying at Dan's house when the raid took place. He firmly opposed duelling, but he knew his nephew's honour was at stake. He was

furious with Mary for intervening: 'Mary, this is the only time in my life I ever was angry with you, and you have made me very angry.'

Mary was unrepentant, and assured the old general: 'I would much rather vex you than let my husband be killed.'

Colonel Samuel Brown, Peel's new second, became annoyed at the delay. Dan let him know that it was his wife who had caused the distraction, and it was resolved that they should make for the Continent to avoid any further arrests or interventions.

The duel was thus arranged for Ostend in Belgium. And so, on the morning of Thursday 7 September 1815, Dan set out from Dublin for Killarney with Mary. The idea of the long journey was to give his wife a break in Kerry. He would then trick her into thinking he was setting out for legal work in Cork. The ruse worked, and he left her calm and unsuspicious while he made for Waterford with his brother James. They were bound to board the next packet ship and strike for Europe.

The whole matter of travel was a challenge in itself. From the time Dan left Dublin with Mary it took ten days to reach London, by way of horse-drawn carriage and packet ship. After a bothersome journey through south Wales, the small delegation of Dan, his brother James and Richard Newton Bennett reached Cheltenham on Saturday 16 September 1815. At least fifteen hours on the road lay ahead of them as they set off for London, where they finally arrived the next day. Like a prizefighter awaiting the challenge of his life, Dan armed himself with positive thoughts. It was from Cheltenham he wrote to Denys Scully: 'It is perhaps absurd, but I cannot bring myself even to doubt success.'

Peel was already in Ostend practising his marksmanship when Dan prepared to leave London for the port of Dover. The officers at Bow Street police station had been doing their homework, however, and as soon as Dan attempted to board his carriage, Chief Magistrate Nathaniel Conant stepped forward and arrested him. Together with Peel's father, who had offered a reward for Dan's arrest, the Home Office was determined to prevent the duel.

Conant and forty constables escorted Dan to Bow Street station. There he was assured that if he or Peel continued their quarrel, and if either man died, the culprit would be executed. It was there, in central London, the matter ended. Dan was dejected, and later wrote to Scully:

'My heart is still very sore. The scoundrels ... what a glorious opportunity they have deprived me of.'

Although Dan had escaped from Mary in Killarney, he knew he would now have some explaining to do, such was the huge coverage granted to the affair in the newspapers. When he eventually got back to Dublin he wrote her a letter, telling her about the horrible journey back. He was attempting to win her over by gaining some sympathy:

Not a berth could be had for love or money. I lay on the cabin floor as sick as a dog, with three gentlemen's legs on my breast and stomach, and the sea water dripping in on my knees and feet. I was never so completely punished.

The Ascendancy leadership continued to mock Dan, and little ditties and satirical poems about his wife's command over him did the rounds.

History, however, would remember the fatal shot to D'Esterre, and by the time his greatest challenges to the Empire came around Dan's honour would be intact. The blood that had stained the snow at Bishop's Court would be remembered both by those who saw it and by those who read about it in the papers. There would never again be an 'unfavourable impression' about Dan's courage. He was now a man to be reckoned with.

CHALLENGING TIMES: 1816–22

While Dan continued to struggle in his great quest for Emancipation, problems for the rural Catholic poor were getting worse.

The second decade under the Union had seen small benefits for some Irish farmers, but it was a time of distress for the vast majority of the people. When Napoleon was defeated at Waterloo in 1815 – ending the Napoleonic Wars – demand for agricultural produce from Ireland declined. The prices for barley and beef, for example, fell by more than a half. Now the farmers were struggling to make ends meet, with cottiers and labourers falling into absolute poverty. The survival of the poorest was being made impossible due to unemployment, high rents, forced payment of tithes and evictions.

All around the country, underground illegal societies such as Whiteboys, Ribbonmen, Caravats and Rockites were out at night to fight this injustice. The most disturbed areas were in the west and south-west. The cattle of wealthy landowners and farmers were mutilated, houses were burned and weapons were stolen, wherever they could be found.

In Tralee, in the spring of 1816, Dan worked a vicious court session, where seven men were convicted of serious crimes. 'I really believe they will all be executed,' he wrote to his eleven-year-old daughter Ellen. In another incident in Louth, eighteen men *were* executed, after being accused of killing a landlord and his family at Wildgoose Lodge. The bodies of the eighteen dead were strung up for all to see, and were left to rot for two years.

87

Punishment differed from district to district, depending on the judge. At the spring assizes of 1817, for example, Judge Mayne in Limerick regularly handed down sentences of hanging for house robberies. Three men caught in possession of guns were sentenced to a whipping through the streets of Kilrush, as was a man who had handled stolen goods.

As trouble escalated and poverty increased, Robert Peel's Peace Preservation Force was deployed. This regiment was set up in 1814 by the Chief Secretary when disturbances in the countryside had begun to get out of control. The Force proved very unpopular with the gentry of the disturbed districts, however, as they had to pay for the extra manpower.

Nonetheless, rural violence was at such high levels that on one occasion the Force and up to 12,000 troops had to act in a disturbed district in County Tipperary. Other areas, like County Donegal, saw the Force deployed to counter the illegal manufacture of alcohol, which was widespread.

It was in this climate of fear, violence and crime that Dan continued his rounds on circuit. Terribly cold inn rooms in small towns and villages provided him with what little rest he could find in the busy seasons. He had occasion to be fearful himself. Once, outside Nenagh, he readied himself to use his own gun.

The Tipperary town and its surrounds were swarming with organised rural terrorists, the so-called *banditti*. One morning, as he trundled along in his horse-drawn carriage, Dan spotted a man dressed in black slowly and suspiciously crossing the puddled road. Dan's horses, which were becoming old and haggard, slowed as they approached. The stranger then rested against a wall and laid his hand in the breast pocket of his coat. Dan felt certain he was done for, and so cocked his pistol and placed his finger on the trigger. As the vehicle passed slowly by, the stranger stood still and silent, like a roadside statue. 'Had he but raised his hand, I would have fired,' Dan later said. Such was the danger to life on the road at this time.

Dan had little choice but to work the circuits, still barred as he was from the higher ranks of his profession, and now desperately seeking

88

funds to manage his accumulating debts. He worked tirelessly. His diary over that spring of 1816, for example, records him working the Limerick court all day one Sunday until midnight. After a little sleep, he set out for Tralee at five in the morning, not arriving there until nine that night. Needless to say he was exhausted, having slept very little.

Tired and overworked as he was, Dan was known throughout the land. Since the killing of D'Esterre, and his apparent willingness to kill Chief Secretary Peel, he had become something of a folk hero. As a result, he made considerably more money on circuit in these times than any other barrister. Even so, there was more money going out than coming in. His disastrous financial business with a Mr James O'Leary had been top gossip in Kerry.

Dan's quarrel with Hunting Cap had been miraculously resolved in 1806 when he saved his uncle from an embarrassing prosecution, after a large consignment of brandy had been found at Derrynane. But if Hunting Cap heard of Dan's involvement in this affair with Mr James O'Leary he would have finally disinherited his nephew. Fearing the worst, Dan's sister Ellen placed two men on watch at Derrynane. Their duty was to ask visitors not to mention the matter to old *Caipín*.

In truth, it wasn't just O'Leary whom Dan had to blame for his escalating money problems. He himself was loose and careless with his shillings, even when his purse was virtually empty, for he was fond of extravagance. He sent his children to the finest schools and splashed out wildly for his house on Merrion Square. A man about town needed a fine mode of transport, and so he spent lavishly on an opulent carriage with the O'Connell crest emblazoned on the doors.

Mary scolded him for spending so much on the luxurious Dublin house, when something humbler would do. And yet, she too was guilty of financial foolishness. Although Dan was earning much more than his colleagues on circuit, he still owed up to four times his annual earnings. Mary suggested they ought to 'trespass a little' on savings they were trying to build up. The object of this 'trespass' was a grand piano she had her eye on!

Their income was bolstered by rents from tenants of their Derrynane lands. But when disaster struck for the peasantry in 1816, this too began to dry up. It was known as 'the year without a summer', after a volcanic eruption in Asia caused bad weather around the world. The result in Ireland was a summer and autumn marked by little sun and heavy rainfall. The crops failed. There were reports of ducks swimming among the oats and potatoes in the flooded fields. It was the start of the first major Irish famine in almost a hundred years. The distress of hunger, as well as the onset of typhus, would last until 1819 and result in the deaths of some 65,000 people.

'The times are very distressing to the country,' said Dan, while travelling by coach through Munster. 'There is no prospect of alleviation.'

There was to be no remedy for the widespread hunger for up to a year, after which time Robert Peel got access to some funds to help relieve the poor.

Hunting Cap, too, fell foul of the misery, and was laid up in bed for much of September 1816. As the long nights closed in, Dan was forced to stay indoors with his ailing uncle. The never-ending rain had ruined the autumn festival at Cahirciveen, a day Dan had looked forward to with schoolboy excitement. Worse still, he noted from his room at Derrynane, the misfortune of the times was ruining the peasantry.

'The rents are coming very slowly,' he wrote to Mary, 'and between the fall of prices and the dreadful weather there is nothing but rain and wretchedness.'

During these dire times, Dan turned to God. He had killed a man only a year before, an incident that increasingly troubled him. He had diced with death in challenging Peel, only to be saved from himself by outside forces. His debts were getting out of hand, and he now toiled endlessly in an effort to control them. On top of all this, he was watching his people, the ever-increasing population of Irish Catholics, struggling to survive in the most miserable conditions.

Dan decided to get instruction and guidance from a clergyman, F. J. L'Estrange. He began to attend Mass regularly, prayed often, and fasted during Lent and on Fridays. He became so devout that during the assizes of the Lenten period he refused to eat, no matter the duration of the court sessions, much to the consternation of his wife:

'I fear you are observing Lent too strictly,' said Mary. 'To be from nine o'clock in the morning to perhaps ten at night without a morsel, in a cold courthouse, is more than any constitution (however good) will be able to bear.'

'I am as well,' replied Dan, 'as any man in Ireland ... It fatigues me sometimes a little but it agrees perfectly with me, and I eat on abstinence days an enormous amount of fish.'

So powerful had his faith become that in one incident in March 1817 he feared for his life if a priest could not be found. He had just got off a boat in north Wales when he developed a deathly fever. 'I was not consoled by reflecting,' said Dan, 'that should my illness threaten life, there was no Catholic priest within 40 miles.'

It was not the first time he had been struck with such a malady and, equally, his wife was feeling rather brittle that spring. Mary suffered from cough and chest troubles over the years and, by this time, at the age of thirty-seven, she had already given birth to nine children. She seldom complained of her health and during the assizes her letters to Dan held little or no complaint.

But on his return to Dublin in April, Dan noticed an acute difference in her. She was in visibly poor health. The solution they came up with was to take Mary to the town of Clifton in England, where the bathing waters were said to have great healing powers. On arrival she immediately perked up, and in the presence of her children and their governess, Miss Gaghran, she began to enjoy wandering the markets of Bristol, a short walk from their lodgings.

After fifteen years of marriage Dan's love for Mary had not diminished; it had only strengthened. He consulted her about everything, and during times when they were apart, like this, he wrote to her on subjects ranging from the trivial, to aggregate meetings, to Robert Peel.

On the topic of Peel, it was time for Dan to return to London. He had been bound to keep the peace ever since the affair of honour between the two. The officer who arrested Dan, Nathaniel Conant, wanted this bond renewed, and so a trip to the English capital was necessary. Defending himself, Dan won the pardon of the judge and was discharged.

While in London, Dan went to the House of Commons with his friend the Knight of Kerry. They were walking through the lobby – in fact, they were standing right on the spot where Spencer Perceval had been murdered in 1812 – when suddenly a man in a blue coat rushed past. He bumped off Dan's shoulder. Dan turned around to see that the man was none other than Peel himself. They eyeballed each other, before moving swiftly on. It was the closest, physically, the foes would ever come to one another.

Dan later took time out to catch a performance of Shakespeare's play *All's Well That Ends Well* at the Drury Lane Theatre. The greatest actor of the day, Edmund Kean, played a starring role. Dan wasn't much impressed: 'I do not so much admire Kean. He played Bertram. There was only once a burst to justify his fame.'

Nor was he much impressed by the many leading English figures he met and dined with. Indeed, he frowned upon what he saw as their limited talents: 'I felt how cruel the Penal Laws are which exclude me from a fair trial with men whom *I look on* as so much my inferiors.'

These were the thoughts that were with Dan as he made his way back across England via Oxford, Stratford-upon-Avon and Holyhead.

Back in Dublin, the squabbling among the Catholic Association members did little to help the cause. Already, in that spring of 1817, Dan had gatecrashed a meeting at which the vetoists (those in favour of the 'securities' that included giving the King power to appoint Catholic bishops) had planned to go behind his back. They were in the process of sending a petition for Catholic Emancipation, with securities, to London with Henry Grattan.

As the vetoists were meeting in the private residence of a nobleman, they imagined no one would dare to intrude on their privacy. But, lo and

93

behold, in the midst of preparing their delegates for London, there came a loud and repeated thud on the front door.

Chevalier de McCarthy was braver than the rest and jumped up, rushing to see who was making the racket. No sooner had McCarthy returned to the drawing room, whispering in the ears of his men, when in burst Dan. He bounded up to the meeting table with a look of scorn.

He began to abuse all present. He told them that the Catholics who were against the veto were their superiors in every aspect. He noted that the biggest problem for the Catholic cause was the division among its leaders. When he proposed a new Catholic committee, made up of men from both squabbling sides, he was voted down by the vetoists. He then rebuked those around the table, telling them their cause was ridiculous. They had, he assured them, 'miserable support, against the universal voice of Ireland'.

So, with a split in the camp and a hopeless apathy hanging over the country, the Catholic Association was making no progress. Dan was paying the rent of its offices on Capel Street out of his own pocket. With his personal debt crisis, and now his life's passion in danger of running aground, this was one of the most difficult periods in his life. 'With the exception of himself,' his son later said, 'scarce anyone was in the field for Ireland.'

Dan wrapped up the Association, but soon began a new Catholic Board. Alas, nothing changed, and after this new Board began quickly running up large debts, it too was wrapped up that winter.

The general apathy on the question of Catholic rights continued into 1818 and no petition was sent forward to London. The year did mark Robert Peel's departure as Chief Secretary, however. As the champion of the Protestant elite, his exit offered some kind of hope. His successor, Charles Grant, at least said that he was committed to the Catholic question.

94

At this stage the typhus epidemic that had been put in motion by the famine of 1816 was worsening. Early in 1819, the House of Commons appointed a Select Committee to enquire into the state of disease and rampant poverty throughout Ireland.

As the population continued to grow, the patches of land being used to feed more and more families were getting smaller and smaller. Dan addressed the issue of Catholic grievances in the newspapers on New Year's Day 1819, something that was to become a regular occurrence in the following years. Henry Grattan again petitioned Parliament, in yet another effort to push the cause, but again the motion was defeated. Ireland was choking under the foot of English rule and freedom looked a long way off.

Exhausted by the struggle and seemingly alone 'in the field for Ireland', as his son had put it, Dan began to take great inspiration from the struggles of another towering leader. Simón Bolívar, known as The Liberator, or *El Libertador* in his native Venezuela, was attempting to free his country from Spanish rule. In July 1819 Dan organised a dinner in Dublin's Morrison's Hotel to support Bolívar's cause. On the morning before the dinner Dan had been injured when he was thrown from his horse while dashing through the Phoenix Park, but he was determined to make the event, and so hobbled along regardless.

John Devereux was guest of honour on the night. A tall, handsome Wexford adventurer, he had fought for Irish freedom during the 1798 Rebellion. After spending time in the United States, he had ventured south and agreed to help Bolívar in his cause. Now Devereux was back in Dublin to raise an Irish legion for the South American freedom fighter.

Dan allowed his fifteen-year-old son Morgan to be thrust forward after he requested to join the ranks. Morgan was swiftly and nobly commissioned by the visiting Devereux. It was to be the young man's first worldly adventure, and, in August 1820, he met Bolívar himself after stepping ashore at Barranquilla in Colombia. There the young O'Connell presented Bolívar with a letter from his father, which read:

95

Illustrious Sir,

A stranger and unknown, I take the liberty of addressing you. I am encouraged to do so by my respect for your high character and by my attachment to that sacred cause which your talents, valour and virtue have gloriously sustained ~ I mean the cause of liberty and national independence ...

Your Excellency's most obedient, most faithful, humble servant,

Daniel O'Connell

After reading Dan's letter, Bolívar assured Morgan he would always be the young man's friend and protector, happy to do anything in his power for him.

The young captain or, as he proudly signed off his letters, 'Morgan O'Connell, Lieutenant and Aide-de-Camp', did not see battle. He proved his valour in other ways. On a roundabout voyage home, for instance, he was shipwrecked twice along the Tongue of the Ocean in the Bahamas, before having to fend off a knife attack from a delirious ship's officer at St Jago de Cuba. In the Caribbean he had met an old seaman who turned out to be a never-before-seen, long-lost relative. Yet they had no sooner met than the old wanderer, Charles O'Connell, died of a heart attack in young Morgan's arms.

Morgan finally made it back to Dublin after joining an England-bound Navy warship, *The Raleigh*. Although it was a needless expedition for the young man, and almost proved fatal, Dan was somewhat defiant, saying it had done Morgan nothing but good.

Dan, of course, had his own great love for adventure, and he continued to spend his late summers on the Derrynane hills, hunting with his beagles. As he did after any good season on the Kerry Mountains,

Dan struck back for Dublin in the autumn of 1819 with a spring in his step. 'I never was in half such spirits on political subjects,' he told Mary, and he hoped the next sessions of Parliament would prove helpful to the Catholic cause.

A year of great preparation came to nothing, however, when Grattan, armed with a number of petitions, fell ill and died in London in June 1820. The petitions were never presented in the House of Commons. Despite Dan's differences with Grattan, he paid the deceased a great tribute by saying he had been 'the greatest man Ireland ever knew'. However, in this moment of gloom, Dan considered another missed chance: 'The best opportunity I have ever known of pressing for Emancipation on the ministry has been thrown away and lost forever.'

But something unforeseen occurred the following March while Dan was out on circuit. The MP William Plunket petitioned Parliament with a bill favouring Catholic Emancipation. Unlike the previous years, when failure was taken for granted, the bill passed through the Commons. However, it failed the tougher test in the House of Lords and was defeated by 159 votes to 120.

In the bill Plunket had handed over, 'securities' again would have allowed the Government to appoint Catholic bishops. Dan was raging that Plunket had gone behind his back.

'I would infinitely rather perish with disgrace on a scaffold than assent to such a law,' he fumed.

Nonetheless, a bill for Catholic Emancipation had finally received a majority vote in the House of Commons, and so 1821 marked the emergence of some kind of hope.

Not long before this, the Prince of Wales had taken formal power as King, after his father, George III, passed away. The Prince thus became King George IV. The new monarch decided to make a royal visit to Ireland shortly after his coronation in the summer of 1821. When he disembarked from the royal steamer at Howth, the new King was in an unsteady condition. His wife, Caroline, had passed away only a week before, and it seemed the King drank his way across the Irish Sea. Nonetheless his visit to Ireland was a success.

The Corporation of Dublin had proposed that Protestants and Catholics should show a united front upon the King's arrival. Dan decided to agree. He felt a spirit of friendship would be the best way to help the Catholic cause. The King was greeted with banners that read 'A hundred thousand welcomes' on his way through Dublin's city centre, where throngs of people had lined the streets. The royal procession of carriages and horsemen was estimated to be a mile long.

After a number of grand banquets and days at the Curragh races, the King's visit ended at Dún Laoghaire, where Dan presented him with a crown of laurels. Dan received much criticism for the respect he had given to such an inept and anti-Catholic King. As Dan himself had said some years before: 'There never was a greater scoundrel.'

To explain his actions, Dan said he would always be loyal to the monarchy, no matter who was King or Queen. He wanted Ireland to have its own Parliament in Dublin, but he also wanted it to remain a 'limb of the empire'. Thus, he had offered the hand of friendship and respect to the new King.

And so Dan continued to long for a peaceful resolution to Ireland's problems. He did not want victory – Emancipation or Repeal – to be won through violence. A peaceful revolution had just swept through Portugal. He said these events filled him with hope: 'What is most consoling is that all these great changes are taking place without bloodshed. Not one human life sacrificed, no plunder, no confiscation ... what every honest man must approve of.'

Rural Ireland, however, remained a hotbed of violence, and as a defence counsel in many court cases Dan was right in the thick of it. After one particularly brutal crime in Limerick, he defended a man named Paddy Dillane, who had led a gang of Whiteboys in the killing of Thomas Hoskins at Newcastle West. Hoskins was the son of a barbarous land agent of the Courtenay estate who had locked himself away out of fear of the peasantry. On a country lane, an undercover Dillane and his accomplices pulled the young Hoskins off a mule and shot him three times. As he lay dying in the mud, the Whiteboys danced around him for an hour while one played a tune on the fife.

During the trial, in the autumn of 1822, Dillane admitted to Dan that he was the original 'Captain Rock'. He told Dan he had been given the title by a schoolteacher after his accuracy at throwing rocks had become local legend. He went on to inform on his accomplices, a decision that forced him to leave Ireland, but 'Captain Rock' lived on. During a spate of rural violence from 1821 to 1824, notes and death threats to landlords and tithe collectors were signed off 'Captain Rock'. He had become the phantom leader of a new secret society known as the Rockite movement. Over a hundred Rockites were hanged in this period, with hundreds more transported.

Dan defended many of those standing trial, sometimes on charges of the most vicious crimes. Even though he condemned secret societies and brutal violence, he was still worshipped by the Catholic peasantry in these troubled spots. These rural poor, with many of the *banditti* among them, not only saw Dan as the man who defended them, they also saw him as the man who would eventually liberate them.

What sharpened this belief was a pamphlet widely circulated at the time, containing the prophecies of one 'Signor Pastorini' – actually an English Catholic bishop, Charles Walmesley – which promised the violent destruction of the Protestant Church in 1825.

Dan criticised the pamphlet, saying it was badly written, without 'taste or talent'. Even so, many in the huts and cabins throughout rural Ireland saw Dan as the leader of the movement to rid Ireland of the Protestant Ascendancy. It was a following Dan would tap into in the next great chapter of his life.

BIRTH, DEATH AND DEFEAT: 1823–5

Two years had passed since George IV's visit to Dublin. There had been little or no improvement for Ireland's Catholics in the meantime, despite the welcome the King had received. In response, the Whiteboys and the Rockites had been out and about the countryside – pillaging and destroying Protestant houses, and burning Protestant churches – in retaliation for the injustices and bleak conditions the poor were suffering.

It was in the middle of this unrest that Dan and an old opponent, Richard Sheil, met at Glencullen House on 8 February 1823, and decided to resolve their differences. The new Catholic Association was born. Casting aside the bigger question of Emancipation, the new Association's

objective in the early days was to represent the people. It was to be a body to listen to the grievances of the poor, and assist in whatever way it could.

Initially, during the first meetings at Dempsey's Tavern in Dublin, some of the new board members objected to the change of approach. Many of the upper-class Catholics wanted the Association to concentrate on Emancipation. However, the immense poverty and the violence terrorising the countryside needed an immediate solution.

'First, some persons must take the trouble of managing the affairs of the Catholics,' Dan told one of the Association's first meetings, on 25 April 1823.

The old grievances of tithe payments, high rents, evictions by landlords and rigged court trials had heightened the anger among the people. As well as representing the common Catholics, Dan's aim for the Association was simply 'to take the strongest measures the law will allow to force our cause on the attention of Parliament'.

Dan proposed that members of the Association pay one guinea per year as a subscription. He welcomed, even encouraged, people of every other religious persuasion to attend the meetings. These members would not be charged. Catholics, however, needed to pay for the privilege. Some members objected to this, saying it was an injustice that Catholics had not the same rights as Protestants, even here. Dan replied simply that any Catholic who 'did not take a guinea's worth of interest in the Catholic cause' would be 'unworthy' of attending. Protestants, he declared to the critics, were the ones most capable of giving Catholics advice on how to obtain Emancipation.

When one guinea apiece was paid by fifty men on 12 May 1823, the Catholic Association was formally launched. The members at first were made up of the middle and upper classes, such as landowners, barristers, merchants and newspaper editors. A point was made of welcoming reporters, as the Association wanted its meetings reported in detail. Robert Peel, now the Home Secretary, realised the influence of these reports. He noted early on that the publicity these Catholic meetings received more than made up for the small attendances.

After the initial gatherings at Dempsey's Tavern, the Association began using as its headquarters two rooms over Richard Coyne's bookshop on Capel Street. The secretary of the Association was Nicholas Purcell O'Gorman, and he was a stickler for rules and regulations. The 'no house' rule stated that the weekly meetings at three o'clock would be postponed if there was not a minimum attendance of ten people by half past the hour. O'Gorman would almost gloat as he produced his pocket watch at twenty past and placed it on the room's large table. Its tick-

tock infuriated Dan. Six meetings during the first year were adjourned due to this strict behaviour.

On one afternoon, 4 February 1824, Dan sat reading the *Chronicle* newspaper while waiting for the meeting to start. At twenty-seven minutes past three, and still 'no house', he hurled his paper to the floor as O'Gorman stood staring at his timepiece.

Dan had a topic of particular importance he wanted to discuss that afternoon, so he shot down the stairs to collar any stragglers. Inside Mr Coyne's bookshop he spotted three strangers perusing the shelves. As luck would have it the men were priests, and so were automatically honorary members of the Catholic Association. He seized his opportunity. The three clergymen initially resisted his invitation, but after a little cajoling he bundled them up the stairs. O'Gorman was doing a headcount when Dan burst through the door with his small flock. The secretary had to concede defeat.

As soon as the meeting got under way the young priests made a hasty exit, as the rules entitled them to do. After a short introduction by

O'Gorman and the chairman, Fred Conway, Dan stood up. He produced a report entitled 'The Best Mode of Raising a General Subscription throughout Ireland'. He spoke about the census of 1821, and how it had been 'very imperfect'. Even so, he calculated that if only one million of an estimated population of seven million contributed a penny a month to the Catholic cause, the total over a year could easily reach £50,000.

This Catholic 'rent' was to be used in a number of ways. First, it would be used to forward to London the petitions of every Irish county, not only on the subject of Catholic Emancipation, but on every other grievance, of any kind. An agent would be stationed at Westminster to forward such petitions; his payment, too, would come from the fund. Catholics who could not afford the legal costs of defending themselves against Orange Order violence in a court system steeped in Orange principles would also be given financial aid. Funds would be used to educate the poor, for Catholic schools and for the purchase of books. The Catholic clergy would be provided for, in the form of the building of new parochial houses in poor parishes, and by improving their conditions in all aspects of their practice. Money would also be put forward to send priests to North America, where there was a shortage.

One more very important use of the money would be to fund and support a 'liberal press'. The threat of libel always hung over newspapers that supported the Catholic cause. If the Government did not like what the papers printed, it would find a way to bring them to court, and bring about their financial ruin. With money from the Catholic rent, editors would be compensated if they were threatened by the Establishment. Already in Ireland, four of the six main newspapers supported the Catholic cause. Along with *The Freeman's Journal* and the *Dublin Evening Post,* the *Morning Register* and *Weekly Register* were reporting Catholic meetings in minute detail. These publications were passed about and read aloud throughout the country. It was how the Catholic Association spread its message, its ideas and goals. With financial help, the support of these newspapers could be boosted even further.

Most of all, what Dan was proposing would give the people something to be interested in. By giving up their few and scarce coppers, the poor would be committing themselves to a cause. It would finally be a way to do something about their plight.

This crucial meeting over Coyne's bookshop took place with barely a handful of members in attendance, in a cramped room, and was only saved by the brief appearance of three young clerics. Yet the only thing that mattered was Dan's proposal for a Catholic rent. After a committee approved the plan, copies of the report were circulated widely. An edition of Mr Conway's *Dublin Evening Post* gave full details, with rules and regulations of 'The Monthly Catholic Rent'.

The rent began in March and by June there had already been 4,000 collector's books issued to agents the length and breadth of the country. The collection of small regular payments from large numbers of people made it important that local committees were set up. The early days of rent collection focused on local problems. Out of this came a great many political meetings in villages and towns, made up of local Catholics. The countryside became animated at last. No longer was rural violence and revolt the only way to fight the system. Within just a month of its formation Dan was already crediting the Catholic Association with helping to reduce agrarian crime.

Funds began to mount – a trickle at first, but getting larger with each passing month. More importantly, the obvious support Dan was getting from the vast majority of Irish people would put huge pressure on the Government. The new movement was succeeding where all others had failed. The growing 'moral force' of millions threatened the Establishment much more than the violent force of a few. Whereas the Government could subdue violence with more violence, it was much harder to fight a peaceful movement.

For Dan, however, the demands of this new nationwide project, alongside his work on circuit and at the Four Courts, put serious pressure on his schedule. He had little time for leisure, save for a spot of autumn

hunting in the Kerry Mountains. He became rigorous in his habits, intent on getting the most out of his days. Long gone were the lie-ins and the lazy days of youth. Now he was out of bed at 4 a.m., his open fire lit, and he was at his desk by five o'clock. At half past eight one of his daughters would call him for breakfast, when he would sit with his family for an hour. At half past ten he struck out on foot for the Four Courts, a 2-mile walk he covered in twenty-five minutes. Dan made a good habit of being on time, arriving dutifully five minutes before the court proceeded. Without a break, he would work until three o'clock.

On his way from court Dan would stop off at the Catholic Association's office, even when meetings were not taking place. There he would go through the day's letters with the secretary. On arriving back at Merrion Square, he would have his dinner at 4 p.m. and relax with his family. The house was always a magnet for guests and visitors, but once the clock struck half past six, he would retreat to his study, no matter who had called. He would then work until a quarter to ten, when he would go to bed. Dan made a strict rule of being in bed by ten, if the interruptions of travel and public duties could be kept to a minimum. This regime served Dan well and allowed him to get so much done in his life.

And there was *much* to be done. In August 1824, he wrote to Mary from the circuit in Munster lamenting the loss of a court case in which the entire jury was Protestant:

My Catholic client was defeated, but ought not ... I never was more disgusted by the vileness of the bigotry which crushes the Catholics in every step and situation in life.

Dan was becoming ever more popular. When he arrived at the Waterford assizes he was carried by the people about half a mile to his lodgings. While he maintained discipline in his habits in Dublin, life on the road was usually much more hectic. A great dinner was held in his honour in

Waterford, and he did not get to bed until nearly 2 a.m. His horse-drawn carriage spent the next day trundling across Munster, and after twenty-one hours on the road he finally parked up at Killarney at nearly 3 a.m. After only three hours' sleep, he set out again for Tralee for a morning at court. But he refused to complain: 'I went through a good deal of fatigue, but I never was better in health or spirits.'

His vitality and sharp mind were crucial in the courthouse, where he continued to prosper. Peasants destined for the gallows continued to be saved. Larry Cronin, a stout, hardy 25-year-old man, stood in one assize dock accused of burglary. His grisly fate was all but sealed, when suddenly Dan bounded in at a messenger's request. 'Three times the rope seemed tied around poor Larry's neck,' ran one report. 'As many times the dexterity of O'Connell untied the Gordian knot.'

Meanwhile, Robert Peel wanted to be the hangman who strangled the life out of the Catholic Association. In November 1824 he wrote to the Chief Secretary, Henry Goulburn, outlining three ways in which the Association could be put down. The first was to wait for its natural collapse, based on bad management and leadership. The second option was to watch out for any illegal move by the Association, and be ready to pounce. The third was to change the law.

A slip by Dan at a meeting of the Catholic Association in December allowed the forces of the law to move in, and act on the second option. He had told the gathering that if the country were driven mad by persecution, he wished that 'a new Bolívar may be found – may arise – that the spirit of the South Americans may animate the people of Ireland'. Peel used this reported quote to allege that Dan was calling for a violent revolution, and so he was swiftly brought in front of the judges at Green Street Courthouse.

Some of the journalists who had been at the meeting were also called in front of the court. The editor of *The Star* would not allow his reporter to give any evidence against Dan, telling the judge he would not permit his journalists to 'become the accusers of anyone'. The proceedings quickly descended into farce, with one reporter claiming he had kept no notes on Dan's 'Bolívar speech', and his memory could not be trusted. Most embarrassing for the Government was when the reporter for *Saunders' Newsletter,* a Government organ, told the hearing he had dozed off during the speech.

Amid scenes of joking and laughter, the jury threw out the case. It was another triumph for Dan. At the next Catholic Association meeting he was greeted with praise and applause, cheers and waving of hats, which lasted for nearly ten minutes. He stood before the men and issued a statement of defiance. The Catholic Association was, he said, a creature of the Penal Laws. As long as Catholics were denied their rights, then some association would exist to fight for the justice that was rightfully theirs.

If Dan was defiant, the authorities were equally determined. At the opening of Parliament in February 1825, the King, in his speech, implied that the Catholic Association would be put down. The Association was in conflict 'with the spirit of the constitution', George IV said. Dan called a meeting at once in an attempt to prevent this proposed ban. At the same time, he declared the Association's allegiance to the Crown and constitution, and obedience to the law of the land. Despite these declarations of loyalty, Goulburn introduced a new bill for the suppression of 'unlawful societies in Ireland'.

By early 1825 thousands of people had joined the Catholic Association with their penny-a-month contribution. This meant the committee in Dublin was truly a representative body of the whole people of Ireland. This directly breached the Convention Act of 1793, which outlawed any assembly, other than Parliament, chosen to represent the people. Thus, the bill to suppress unlawful societies was brought forward and debated in London.

Meanwhile, back at Derrynane, age was finally catching up with Hunting Cap. At ninety-six, he had already gone half blind, and was terribly frail when he passed away on 10 February 1825. His coffin was

carved from a tree he had felled in his more sprightly days. Dan composed the lines that were etched into his headstone: 'They loved him most who knew him best.'

Dan inherited a large share of Hunting Cap's fortune, as well as the house at Derrynane. The old estate would be the centre of much entertainment and hospitality in the years to follow, but in February 1825 Dan was preoccupied with more pressing matters.

Immediately he had to hasten to London in an effort to defeat the proposed suppression bill. He was initially reluctant to be among the travelling party, as an extended trip would take him from his legal work – and put a sizeable hole in his pocket. The money from Hunting Cap's bequest, however, now allowed him to make the trip.

He set out from Dublin with an entourage that included his son-in-law Christopher Fitzsimon, Richard Sheil, and Thomas Kirwan of the Catholic Association. Dan's personal servant, James, was also in transit. After a rough passage across the Irish Sea, they made their way to London in a carriage via Bangor and Shrewsbury.

Dan was taken aback by the great welcome he received in London. He enjoyed dinners in his honour with leading English Catholics, including dukes, earls and barons. He delighted in the attention, but found they were nevertheless not as passionate about the Catholic cause: 'There is an English coldness; and, after all, what is it to them if we, the Irish Catholics, are crushed?'

While in London he gave evidence on the bad state of Ireland to select committees of both the House of Commons and the House of Lords. He believed these meetings to be a great success and told Mary that the committee members, among them Robert Peel, could not have been more civil or polite. In fact, so delighted was he that he told his wife: 'We have won the game ... I have no doubt that we shall be emancipated.'

While he was in London, Dan drew up a new bill for Catholic relief, and it was with this he hoped to gain Emancipation. The reception he received had encouraged him to feel victory was close at hand. He was now willing to make sacrifices to gain it. After meeting with William Plunket, Dan was convinced to present a bill that had two securities attached. Crucially, they did not include the 'veto' – something Dan had always resented.

One security was the state payment of Catholic clergy, and the other was the loss of votes for the 'forty-shilling freeholders'. This second security meant that, in order to vote, a tenant now needed his land to be worth at least £10. This would mean a dramatic drop in the number eligible to vote. The two securities were known as the 'wings', and Dan believed if they were attached to the relief bill it would fly through both the Houses of Commons and Lords.

Meanwhile, Goulburn had his way and a bill for the suppression of 'unlawful societies' was introduced. It meant the Catholic Association could not meet more than once every fourteen days. The bill was made law on 9 March 1825, and the Association was forced to dissolve itself nine days later.

As many MPs still favoured giving Catholics Emancipation in 1825, Dan's trip to London still had a chance of success. Things appeared to be going according to plan when the Duke of York invited him and his colleagues to a grand function. The Duke was the 'heir presumptive', or the King-in-waiting, and he welcomed the Catholic contingent with the greatest courtesy: 'I would indeed call it kindness,' Dan reported.

But if the Duke was courteous it had nothing to do with his politics. On 25 April 1825 he made a speech at the House of Lords (with tears in his eyes) in which he poured scorn on the Catholic cause. As the Duke was in line to become King, his scathing words had a huge influence on the House.

On the night of 17 May the crucial vote for Emancipation was ready to begin. Dan stood restless in the balcony overlooking the chamber of the

Lords. 'It is *now* or never,' he said. The tension ran until half past five in the morning when, finally, the vote came in. The House of Lords yet again crushed Dan's hopes: it defeated his Emancipation bill by 178 votes to 130. The three-month sojourn in London had been a disaster. Dan had watched as the new Suppression Act was passed, forcing his Catholic Association to disband. He had allowed the much-dreaded 'securities' to accompany his Emancipation bill. And now he watched that same Emancipation bill fall at the last hurdle.

A split again arose among the members of the now former Catholic Association, some of whom criticised Dan's handling of affairs and tactics in London. All the while, Dan had lost a considerable amount of money by neglecting his legal work. He had also spent a sizeable amount of Hunting Cap's legacy. All was not lost, however, for Dan's greatest quality was his optimism.

'We must begin again ... we must never despair,' he wrote to Mary only hours after the crushing defeat at the Lords.

Despite defeat, Dan was given a tremendous ovation when he arrived back at Howth on 1 June 1825. There he was joined by Mary and his daughters, Ellen and Kate. In the city centre, crowds gathered and jostled for position on Sackville Street from midday, awaiting 'the man of the people'. His arrival in the late afternoon was greeted by men waving their hats and women fluttering their handkerchiefs. Dan, in a great blue cloak, saluted the crowd from an open carriage, quite happy to receive the acclaim.

From the balcony of his house on Merrion Square, Dan addressed the multitudes. He urged his fellow Catholics to 'persevere with the spirit of men determined and deserving to be free'. He cried that victory had to be won in a peaceful manner for 'fellowship and good will should be common to all men'. Three great cheers were given for Ireland before the crowds departed.

Thus, in a heartbreaking defeat, an even greater determination was born.

THE ROAD TO EMANCIPATION: 1825–8

Dan had sacrificed much in London, including a great amount of his time and money. While away, however, he had written to Mary and warned her that she must not be angry if he met 'nothing but ingratitude in return'. His words would prove prophetic, and one such critic was a Belfast journalist, Jack Lawless.

He was intent on commenting on the decisions Dan had made at Westminster. At an aggregate meeting on Dan's return, in which he announced plans for getting around the suppression of the Catholic Association, Lawless made an unwelcome appearance. There, in a church on a Dublin side street, he scoffed at Dan's concession of the 'wings'. According to Lawless, accepting the loss of the clergy's independence was bad enough, but allowing for the loss of votes from the forty-shilling freeholders was unacceptable.

The crowd hissed at Lawless. He was soon drowned out and had to retreat. Nonetheless, Dan remained upset by the accusation. He got his chance to remedy the matter some days later when he confronted Lawless at Bridge Street. Lawless was holding a meeting with the hierarchy of his parish to publicly condemn Dan's actions. Dan got wind of the little convention and stormed in, with a troop of his followers quick behind.

There was a great commotion as Dan attempted to take the stage, with Lawless' supporters jeering and whistling. Dan finally silenced the hecklers when he admitted openly to having made mistakes in London. He assured the assembly he had received votes of thanks from almost every county in Ireland for his efforts in the English capital. He also told the meeting he had the support of two very important clergymen, Bishop Doyle and Archbishop Murray.

Bishop Doyle had indeed been in London with Dan – but he was incensed when he heard what Dan had said at Bridge Street. He vehemently denied he had ever agreed to surrender the clergy's independence. He was a young and energetic bishop who had supported Dan's Catholic Association with unusual gusto for a cleric. It was important to keep him happy, so Dan bit his tongue, and asked only that they mend their friendship.

It was at this time that Dan set about resurrecting the Catholic Association. He was determined to find a way around the restrictions imposed by the Suppression Act. Already, in May 1825, he had told Mary of his intentions: 'We must immediately form "the new Catholic Association", I have it all arranged. The Government shall not get one hour's respite from agitation, I promise you ... I never was up to agitation till now.'

There was one loophole in the Suppression Act that Dan was determined to exploit: it exempted 'societies of charity'. So Dan launched the 'New Catholic Association' on 13 July 1825. The movement would exist simply 'for the relief of distressed Catholics'.

As aggregate meetings could now take place only every fourteen days, the new Association called for simultaneous meetings to be held across the country. These meetings would prove to be a striking show of strength from Irish Catholics. Meeting days resembled national bank holidays. On such days, the great swell of Irish peasantry took to the streets of towns and villages, creating one massive voice of dissent against the Government of the day.

No matter the defeats of London, Dan was still the folk hero of the Irish country people. Emancipation would surely come, they believed, having come so close already. After he remounted his carriage in August 1825 and made for the provincial courts, Dan was welcomed by vast crowds in each town. 'It is not possible to convey an idea of his popularity at this juncture,' said William Fagan, a writer from Munster. The people, wrote Fagan, 'loved the man, springing from amongst themselves, who struggled for their freedom'.

During that autumn season Dan took on 'specials', which were court cases outside his usual Munster circuit. One was in Galway, where he was magnificently entertained at a public dinner. Other 'specials' were at Wexford, Newry and Antrim. In Mallow, in County Cork, Dan had to ask the excited crowd that met him to refrain from hoisting his carriage, for the sake of his wife. Mary was in his company and was now in increasingly weak health, coughing and spluttering as the carriage chugged along.

It is a measure of Dan's popularity that even in a year that bore little fruit for Catholic freedom, he was still the people's champion. And he was still a champion of the courtroom. In Cork, two men, Keefe and Burke, were about to face the hangman's noose for the murder of the Franks family. But Dan's defence, and his unequalled powers of cross-examination, saved the men's lives.

Rural violence, while declining, was still a big problem in the southern provinces. The secret society of Ribbonmen had spread from the northern counties, where it had been formed in defence against violent Orangemen. Bishop Doyle, for one, staunchly condemned the actions of the Ribbonmen.

That, however, did not stop young men joining up. In March 1826 Dan wrote to the Attorney General about the growing rural unrest:

One priest told me that no less than seven youths in his parish left his confessional, rather than renounce the system, or abstain from supporting it.

Against this backdrop Dan kept his peaceful Catholic agitation in full swing. He attended country meetings in a uniform he had designed to enhance his stature. He chose to dress as a leader of regal importance. He wore tight white pantaloons (the trousers associated with grand men of the nineteenth century) and a yellow waistcoat, topped off with a great blue cape. His aim during the first months of 1826 was to petition for a new Catholic relief bill. The petition would be prepared to be introduced after the general election that summer, when new members to the House of Commons would be elected.

A major turning point arrived in June when the voters of County Waterford took a stand against the long-dominant Beresford family. The Beresfords were a symbol of the Protestant Ascendancy, and one of the most powerful families in the country. Lord George Beresford had been an MP for Waterford since 1814 and he expected to be re-elected.

The Catholic Association had a good man in that county, though. Thomas Wyse was a local merchant and part of an affluent Catholic family. He was a man of great intelligence and energy. In 1821 he had married Princess Letizia Bonaparte, Napoleon's niece, after meeting her on a trip to the Continent. He now devised a plan to challenge Beresford for his seat at Westminster.

The candidate Wyse chose to run against Beresford was a local Protestant and pro-Emancipationist, Henry Villiers-Stuart. So eager was Villiers-Stuart to accept the call that he hurried back from a holiday in Austria, where a messenger had handed him the request. Wyse worked tirelessly on the campaign, along with a priest, Fr Sheehan. They were helped in their efforts by the parish priests of the county, who preached against Lord Beresford from the pulpits.

With the election fast approaching, Villiers-Stuart invited Dan to Waterford to boost the campaign. He arrived at the Villiers-Stuart residence of Dromana a week before the election. It was a week of travelling throughout the county, arguing the cause for the candidate. One morning on this mini-tour Dan spoke from the window of an inn in the 'Beresford town' of Kilmacthomas. He argued the case against the town's aristocracy in front of the gathered peasantry. 'We had a good deal of laughing at the Beresfords,' Dan would later jest.

Everywhere, the poor locals came out and greeted Dan, Wyse and Villiers-Stuart with green boughs and unimaginable cheers. In a final push against Beresford, it was decided Dan should make a speech at the pre-election political meeting, or 'hustings'. He reminded the crowd surging around him that they had been voting for a system that treated them like slaves. They were electing men, he said, who had enslaved them, and who had enslaved their children, their religion and their country. It was said his speech was one of the most striking ever given, even by him.

Beresford's parliamentary days were numbered. With great organ-isation and efficiency the forty-shilling freeholders were escorted from all around the county to the polling station at Waterford. One by one they cast their vote, and as the hours passed Lord George's grip on his Waterford seat continued to weaken. Villiers-Stuart was leading the contest by 1,357 votes to 527 when Beresford withdrew from the contest.

The freeholders of Waterford had answered the call of Wyse and Fr Sheehan. Their minds had been made up by the words of Daniel O'Connell. Even the tenants of Kilmacthomas had voted for Villiers-Stuart. It was a remarkable victory, and the spirit of revolt in Waterford spread to Armagh, Louth, Monaghan and Westmeath, where similar pro-Emancipation victories were recorded.

The tenant revolt was not without its consequences, however. As Dan rushed back to Dublin to his ailing sweetheart Mary, many of the rebellious freeholders were feeling the wrath of their landlords. Evictions occurred, privileges were withdrawn and any rents in arrears were demanded at once.

Yet Wyse and Fr Sheehan had foreseen such a development and had come up with a response to such punishment long before the election. A local fund, providing both money and alternative land, was set up for any freeholder against whom a landlord had retaliated. Likewise, the Catholic Association launched the 'new' Catholic rent in July to assist tenants facing demands on rent arrears. The tenants, said Dan, 'made great sacrifices and it was right they should be protected'.

The election successes of Waterford and the other counties had given the people new energy. They saw that the Catholic Association could influence who was voted into Government. The cause had been reawakened, and the new rent was the driving force that allowed the people to get involved. Dan had also been revived by a lengthy break at Derrynane during the autumn, and he returned to Dublin with a renewed fighting spirit:

119

'Temperateness, moderation and conciliation are suited only to continue our degradation,' he told the Knight of Kerry. 'If we want to succeed, we must speak out boldly, and rouse in Ireland a spirit of *action*.'

The 'action' Dan focused on during 1827 was a renewed effort to collect the Catholic rent, with the help of the clergy. Indeed, he regularly contributed his own money, with monthly donations sent forward from whatever assize town he happened to be in. He was unhappy overall by the returns of the Catholic rent, which averaged just £100 per week during 1827. At the end of the year the Association created a new 'churchwarden' system. In each parish two churchwardens were appointed to carry out the work of the Catholic Association at ground level. Their task was to select people to collect the Catholic rent and to supervise the collection. The wardens would also report on evictions, and any other issues, to the central body in Dublin.

With the work of the churchwardens, the Catholic Association now had managers in each parish. Its success was immediate: the first week of the warden scheme saw the rent rise to £604. Not only that, but the wardens were getting locals involved in the work. The whole scheme had become infinitely stronger.

However, the vigour of the Catholic Association in Ireland in 1827 was not matched by success in London's Parliament. With a new Government in place following the election, the English politician Sir Francis Burdett brought forward a motion in favour of Catholic Emancipation on 5 March 1827. The proposal was rejected in the House of Commons by just four votes, much to Dan's fury. One week later, at a Catholic meeting in Ennis, he warned all future election candidates to support Emancipation or face not getting a single vote from his followers.

Despite Government opposition to Emancipation in 1827, it was to be a year of great change in the administration. One of the biggest opponents of Emancipation, the Duke of York, died in early January. Only one month later the anti-Catholic Prime Minister, Lord Liverpool, suffered a brain haemorrhage that put him out of office for good. The King then chose

George Canning to take over the role of Prime Minister. Strangely, Canning too was in very poor health. At the Duke of York's funeral, he – along with several others – fell severely ill in an unheated chapel. Dan supported Canning during his brief term in office in the belief the new Prime Minister would back Emancipation. Canning, though, did little for the Catholic cause, and died on 8 August. A short spell then followed during which Lord Goderich, Frederick Robinson, entered 10 Downing Street. His only notable contribution as Prime Minister was to spend lavishly on his new home, before being dismissed in January 1828.

All the while, the Catholic Association, although still under the Suppression Act, was enjoying its revival. After the churchwarden scheme had been brought in, and only weeks before Lord Goderich left Downing Street, simultaneous meetings were held in 1,600 of the 2,500 parishes in Ireland on Sunday 13 January. Over one and a half million people came out of their hovels and cabins that morning to support the cause.

'The combination of national action – all Catholic Ireland acting as one man – must necessarily have a powerful effect on the minds of the ministry and of the entire British nation,' said Dan. 'A people who can be brought to act together and by one impulse are too powerful to be neglected, and too formidable to be long opposed.'

The one man Dan feared could oppose such action was the Duke of Wellington, and it was he who replaced Lord Goderich as Prime Minister on 22 January. Wellington had led the forces that defeated Napoleon in the European war. Dan had already said that if the Duke assumed power 'all the horrors of actual massacre threaten us'.

121

But Dan was wrong. The Government formed by Wellington and his new Home Secretary, Robert Peel, would oversee the most triumphant period in Dan's career up to that point. An old, battle-hardened comrade of Wellington's, Lord Anglesey, joined the administration as the new Lord Lieutenant of Ireland. Anglesey had been an ultra-Protestant, but had begun to soften towards the Catholics. Wellington's Cabinet was also far from anti-Catholic, with seven of thirteen members being pro-Emancipation.

Nonetheless, the Catholic Association vowed to oppose all future election candidates unless they were in opposition to Wellington's Government. Hostility to the administration increased when some of the pro-Emancipists withdrew from Cabinet in May. With these departures a number of positions had to be filled.

William Vesey Fitzgerald, MP for County Clare, was promoted, and as a result he was required to be re-elected to his Clare seat. Although he was a popular landlord, Fitzgerald was a member of Wellington's administration, and so the Catholic Association decided instantly to oppose him. Two Catholic Association members from Clare, Tom Steele and the extravagant James O'Gorman Mahon, went to Ennis in pursuit of a suitable candidate.

Steele and 'The O'Gorman Mahon', as he titled himself, proceeded to jaunt about the county, going from village to village proclaiming that victory was theirs if they could find a candidate. By the end of their canvass, however, the two squireens were still without a man to go forward. Nonetheless, O'Gorman Mahon struck for Dublin with news of the faithful Clare support.

Already, back in the capital, a prominent merchant and supporter of the Catholic Association, David Roose, had come up with a startling idea: he believed Dan himself should run for the vacant seat. There was no law against Catholics running for election. But the Protestant oaths they would be required to take on entering Parliament prevented them from doing so. Roose believed that such was the force of the agitation in

122

Ireland, led by Dan, that he was sure to be elected. Then, if he was not allowed to enter Parliament, it was believed a rebellion, like 1798, would soon follow. Surely, thought Roose, the Government must give in. Later that day, he encountered Dan's close friend P. V. FitzPatrick on a Dublin street, and told him about the idea. FitzPatrick wandered off, thunderstruck by the audacity of the plan. He murmured to himself: 'Great God, the Catholics are at last emancipated!'

Dan had already been thinking of running, and when FitzPatrick approached him the wheels were put in motion. He briefly hesitated at taking on the daunting challenge, and wondered if he had enough money to fund a campaign. But FitzPatrick was adamant and vowed to raise the money himself. The offer was not needed, for when Dan finally announced the challenge for the Clare seat the Catholic Association put £5,000 into a fund for election expenses. Donations of £100 each from a number of wealthy Catholics also boosted the fund. The path was now clear for Dan to strike for Ennis.

By the evening light of Saturday 28 June 1828, Dan was working his way through the countryside toward Clare, continuing on through the black of night. His carriage was drawn by six great mares. The flicker of rushlight brightened every cabin window. Together with Nicholas Purcell O'Gorman and Richard Newton Bennett, Dan greeted the peasantry, who lit the roads with bonfires in celebration.

While Dan worked his way west, the *Dublin Evening Post* was coming hot off the printing press. Dan's intentions were outlined clearly in black and white:

It is true that as a Catholic I cannot, and of course never will, take the oaths at present prescribed to Members of Parliament; but the authority which created these oaths, the Parliament – can abolish them ... If you elect me, the most bigoted of your enemies will see the necessity of removing that obstacle.

Dan intended to force his way into Parliament by making the King remove the oaths. It was in this combative mood that he crossed the Shannon into Clare. He had already made his way through a host of Masses, gallant speeches and outbursts of acclaim in places like Roscrea, Nenagh and Toomevara. Exhausted, he and his small entourage finally reached the square in Ennis in the early hours of Monday 30 June. The townspeople had waited up to greet 'the great Dan'. Sleep could wait when such a national event was happening in one's own district. Indeed, the result of the Clare election was awaited by audiences not only in Ireland and London, but across Europe.

There was to be little rest for Dan either, as the official nominations had to be handed in at the Ennis courthouse at 11 a.m. It was Vesey Fitzgerald, however, who got the first points on offer. He and his entourage, made up of almost all the county's gentry, had arrived early, and they promptly took up all the best seats. When Dan bustled in his face was bright, however. He joked that he was only too happy to stand with 'the people'. His words were met with boisterous cheering from his fiery supporters.

Vesey Fitzgerald was then nominated by his friend Sir Edward O'Brien, who, in a rant, charged that if Dan were elected County Clare would not be a fit place to live in. Vesey Fitzgerald then took the platform and won over the crowd as he spoke, in a flood of tears, about his ill father. His tears were genuine, but Dan was both bold and brutal in his reply: 'I have wept over my lot in private, but I never shed my tears in public,' spat Dan.

Fitzgerald began to feel faintly embarrassed. Dan then castigated him for being a friend of Wellington's. The Duke, declared Dan, was only a stuttering, confused and incomprehensible speaker. The abuse continued, as Dan labelled Vesey Fitzgerald as a man 'who suppressed the Catholic Association'. As Dan piled further insult on Fitzgerald and the Government, he was greeted with loud shouts and cheering. The courthouse was united in his favour.

Up to 3,000 troops had been deployed outside to keep order on the streets, which were filling by the hour. The forces were scarcely needed, as right from Dan's arrival, the town was a place of joy and excitement, with not so much as a hint of violence. He had sent out two general orders: there was to be no drinking and no physical disturbance. A German traveller and Prince, Mr Puckler-Muskau, was in the town and he noted the punishment dished out to a youth for breaking the first order:

'A delinquent was thrown into a certain part of the River Fergus, and held there for two hours, during which time he was made to undergo frequent submersions.'

In this way a 'delinquent' learned his lesson by almost drowning, or from embarrassment, or both.

'We were watching the movement of tens of thousands of disciplined fanatics,' said Robert Peel. 'They were abstaining from every excess and every indulgence, and concentrating every passion and feeling on one single object.'

125

The organisation for the election took its lead from Waterford two years previously. Great crowds of men, women and children flocked from the townlands of the county. Kitchens and accommodations were set up. Speeches were made. Masses were said. To the packed square, one priest announced that a forty-shilling freeholder who had voted against Dan had just dropped dead. The crowd fell silent, gasping as one, before kneeling in solemn prayer.

Another priest, Fr Maguire, convinced Vesey Fitzgerald's own tenants to walk away from their landlord and vote for Dan. They answered the call, leaving Vesey Fitzgerald in a flood of tears as they marched to the polling booth. It was the priests, 150 of whom were present that week, who were steering the voters in Dan's direction. Fr Murphy of Corofin shouted out to one contingent that was about to vote for Vesey Fitzgerald, 'Men, are ye going to betray your God and your country?'

Dan's popularity, coupled with the pressure to vote for him, made the result a foregone conclusion. By the third day of polling he was already leading by 1,000 votes. At the end of the last day he had crushed Vesey Fitzgerald by 2,057 votes to 982.

Vesey Fitzgerald's agent tried to put a spanner in the works. He declared that Dan's victory was illegal due to the oaths he would never swear in Parliament. But the election assessor said the victory had been won fairly. It was now up to the House of Commons how to proceed.

It was the triumph Dan had been waiting for. He eventually left Ennis after an uproarious ovation from 60,000 supporters, as well as cheers from scores of the Crown troops (many of whom were Catholics). It was exactly what London had feared – Dan's victory in Clare had raised him to the status of 'Liberator' of Ireland. The people had remained quiet and peaceful at his request. Would they go further if he requested it, if he were not allowed to take his seat in Parliament? Wellington and Peel bowed to the inevitable: Catholic Emancipation.

After the election in Ennis, Peel had wondered if there was any sense in repeating such scenes and incurring such risks again. Wellington believed there was not. Already over 80 per cent of the whole of Britain's infantry was in Ireland, and it was still ineffective. Anarchy would follow if the Catholics did not get their way now, and Wellington knew it. He had seen enough bloodshed in his lifetime to know it was time to surrender. King George IV fumed and sulked, demanding concessions. After months of wrangling, disagreements and bickering, he finally conceded defeat. In doing so, he announced bitterly that it was not he, but Dan, who was now 'King of Ireland'.

As he left Ennis on 7 July 1828, Dan must have felt just so. The new Liberator was 'enthroned upon a triumphal car' and mobbed by the multitudes throughout his journey east. Bonfires lit up the nights, while banners, bands, green boughs and leafy wreaths enlivened the days with celebration. On the final leg to Dublin from the Curragh, Dan's horses were unharnessed so the people themselves could draw him along the last few miles.

The result of all those years of struggle was summed up in his favourite quote, by the English poet Lord Byron, in gold lettering on the outside of his carriage:

> Hereditary bondsmen! know ye not
> Who would be free themselves must strike the blow?

THE VICTORY IS SEALED: 1829

The story spread like wildfire. It was said that on Monday 13 April 1829 King George IV, in a fury, had flung his pen to the floor of Windsor Castle and stamped upon it. He had just signed the Catholic Relief Act. Whatever the truth, there was no doubt the King gave the royal assent to Catholic Emancipation reluctantly, and with much bitterness.

'What can I do?' he cried. 'I am miserable, wretched ... If I do give the assent I'll go abroad. I'll not return any more to England.'

But give the assent he did, having bowed in the end to pressure from the Duke of Wellington, as well as from the result of a majority vote in Parliament in favour of Emancipation.

Dan was in London for the news he had waited so long to hear. From his lodgings on Bury Street he wrote to James Sugrue, of the Catholic Association:

The first day of freedom! It is one of the greatest triumphs recorded in history - a bloodless revolution.

He told Sugrue he was now busy making arrangements 'respecting my own seat in Parliament'.

But there was a harsh, unexpected catch to the new Act. Dan had hoped to take the new oaths that had just been drawn up – oaths that were finally acceptable to Catholics. But he had won the election in 1828, when the old oaths were still required. The new oaths, said the King, could not be backdated.

This presented a big problem for Dan when he stepped forward to take his seat as a Member of Parliament in the House of Commons on Tuesday 15 May 1829. If he could not take the new Catholic oaths, he would need to stand for election (and win) again to take his seat. The House chamber was crowded on that fateful day, as all waited to see what would unfold. The Commons in those days was a dark and gloomy hall with no fresh air, which gave rise to intense heat. One journalist even said that on busy days 'the Members were to be pitied'.

It was in this choked atmosphere that Dan presented himself, dressed in black, and flanked by two supporters – Lord Duncannon and Lord Ebrington. When the Speaker ordered Members who wished to take their seats to advance, Dan stepped forward. A hush enveloped the room. The civilians in the overhead galleries craned their necks to get a glimpse of the most unusual sight – a Catholic in the House of Commons. Mr Leys, the House Clerk, then handed Dan three pieces of cardboard containing the old oaths. Dan briefly glanced over them, and in a low voice told the Clerk he could not vow by them. He would take only the new oaths. The Clerk informed the Speaker, who in turn told the House that Dan *had* to swear the old oaths. Nothing else was acceptable. The Speaker ordered Dan to withdraw from his position at the table, but he refused. He stood silent, his gaze fixed on the Speaker.

Mr Henry Brougham, a Whig politician, attempted to speak up on behalf of Dan.

'Order, Order!' shouted the Speaker, as he cracked his gavel.

Finally, Dan bowed and withdrew without uttering, or even attempting to utter, one word. Robert Peel was in attendance, and he insisted that Dan could not speak in the House on that day. Proceedings were adjourned until the following week. It was on 19 May 1829 that the matter finally reached a conclusion.

This time, when Dan stepped in front of the Speaker he was reminded again he must take the old oaths of 1828. Otherwise he would not be permitted to enter Parliament, and there the issue would rest.

'May I ask to see the oath?' enquired Dan. It was a most unusual request. Even so, the Clerk brought forward the card on which that oath was printed. Dan donned his spectacles and perused it intently. The whole chamber sat in silence for several minutes, watching him going over the text. He then broke the silence:

'I see in this oath one assertion as to a matter of fact which I *know* to be false. I see in it another assertion as to a matter of opinion which I *believe* to be untrue. I therefore refuse to take that oath.'

Then, with the deepest contempt, he flung the oath down upon the table. Before a stunned audience and a flummoxed Speaker, his crusade to enter Parliament in 1829 ended there, in spectacular defiance.

A new writ was thus issued for Clare, and an election would take place within weeks. There was nothing for it but to face the expense and exertions of a fresh campaign. 'We must be stirring,' Dan urged Sugrue, only days after his exit from the Commons. While still in London, he drew up a letter to the electors of Clare, which came to be known as the 'address of a hundred promises'. It was published in the *Morning Chronicle* and promised widespread reforms for Ireland.

Even after the latest setback Dan was fully confident of success in the new election, and boarded his return steamer at Holyhead in high spirits. 'I am assured I have a new election quite secure,' he said, shortly before departure. 'I am likely to have a great triumph.'

Like a general returning from his latest battlefield victory, he was welcomed at Howth by a wildly excited crowd. Support for him was never greater, and a fund of £5,000 from the Catholic Association was promptly made available for the contest.

On 7 June 1829 Dan left Dublin for Clare. Enormous crowds greeted him throughout the country, with a particular incident in Limerick summing up the enthusiasm with which he was met. After staying at Moriarty's Hotel in the city, he awoke to an incredible scene. A huge tree had been planted in front of the hotel, and an orchestra had concealed themselves in the thick foliage. Equipped with fiddles and flutes, they began playing national airs when Dan emerged.

With these airs still ringing in his ears, Dan's progress to Clare continued in a carriage drawn by four horses. It was slow going. By the time he reached Ennis, at 1 a.m. on 9 June, his carriage was followed by some 40,000 people. They had struck out on foot from the different districts as soon as his vehicle had been spotted from the brow of a hill or a bend in the road.

Amid this festive spectacle his canvass began. Vesey Fitzgerald was invited to stand again as an opponent, but this time declined; the Clare native held on to a seat he already had for Newport in England. Dan's election was never in doubt, and on 30 July he repeated his victory of 1828. After being escorted throughout the countryside on a 'triumphal chair', he prepared himself for life in London by taking a lengthy sojourn at Derrynane.

During September and October, Dan roamed about the Kerry Mountains, enjoying the sport, the solitude and the fresh air. The bounty on the hills that season was more abundant than ever. 'I never saw better hunting in my life,' he wrote enthusiastically to Mary. But it all nearly ended in tragedy on the side of a steep slope.

Dan was with his brother James as they made their way by mail cart along the Old Coach Road on the great Drung Hill, just outside Kells on the Iveragh Peninsula. When one of the horses stumbled, a harness snapped. In the excitement, the horses took off at full pelt and the dangling carriage was in danger of plummeting down the precipice. The driver shouted, 'Jump out!'

In an instant the brothers threw themselves from the careering cart. Dan landed on his shoulders and was briefly stunned by a smack to the back of his head. When he came around, he found James in a heap on the road, struggling to get up. He had come down on one arm and shattered the bone between the shoulder and elbow.

Dan sprang into action. He sent for surgeons in two directions. He cut up a shirt to make bandages, then tore branches from a tree to make splints for his brother's arm. In no time Dr Barry of Cahirciveen arrived amid a clatter of horses' hooves and quickly attended to the injured James. Dan relayed the whole dramatic incident in an urgent mail to the faithful Mr Sugrue, in which he signed off: 'You may rely, however, on my being in Dublin as speedily as possible.'

Within days, however, a lone horseman appeared at the gates of Derrynane. It was William Burke, who had travelled through the night with the desperate plea from the people of Doneraile (and who we've met already in Chapter 4). For Dan, the man of action, his diary would see another victorious entry for 1829, a year already filled with ups and downs.

And still, some of his greatest challenges were yet to begin.

THE NEW MEMBER OF PARLIAMENT: 1830

Dan was worried he was getting fat. In early 1830 he was fifty-four, and he feared his sedentary habits were making him rather corpulent.

'I care little for your increasing size,' said Mary. 'It can't at all events be unwholesome. You are neither an epicure, nor a hard drinker. You have the best of constitutions and may God continue it to you is my constant prayer.'

The couple wrote to each other with these slight concerns across the Irish Sea. While Mary was at home in Dublin, Dan had made it to London from Holyhead, through a blizzard of sleet and snow.

Whatever about his personal insecurities, as a public man Dan was ready for yet another great moment. The fight had been won; the years of struggle had borne fruit. The obstacles of 1829 had been cleared. He was ready to take his seat for Clare. And so, on Thursday 4 February 1830, he finally walked through the halls of Parliament in confident mood, down towards the candlelit gloom of the House of Commons. Once inside, he shook hands with the Speaker, Charles Manners Sutton. He then swore the amended oaths and took his place in a seat that had been denied Irish Catholics since before the Penal Laws.

Earlier that day the begrudging King had opened the year's session of Parliament in the House of Lords. With the chamber of the House of Commons only half full, Dan was about to begin his parliamentary career by talking about the King's speech. For any debutant, the task of impressing the sitting Members was daunting, but for Dan it was even

more so. Having forced his way into Parliament against the will of so many, his time in the House was going to be a challenge right from the start.

He was looked upon as an intruder. Not only was he an Irish Catholic, he was a passionate one at that. His outbursts and fury towards the Establishment were viewed as undignified and low by the sitting noblemen. Many at Westminster would have gleefully considered duelling with 'the wild Irishman', if only Dan were up for such a challenge. He never was, so determined was he that the D'Esterre incident of 1815 should not be repeated. London's elite considered this mere cowardice. One diarist of the day, Charles Greville, condemned Dan as 'lost to all sense of shame and decency, trampling truth and honour under his feet, cast off by all respectable men'. As an orator, said Greville, Dan was bound to fail in the House of Commons, 'but to a mob, especially an Irish mob, he is perfect, exactly the style and manner which suits their tastes'.

The man of the 'mob' stood up, watched by all with intense curiosity. The great orator began. Dan struck the right chord immediately, and it became clear he could change the tune to suit the audience. His speech was not long, but it was precise and to the point. He told the Speaker he had been sent by the Irish people to 'do their business'. He was intent on making his mark, and straight away began to abuse the King for a speech that was full of 'jejune and empty statements'. He mocked George IV for 'revealing' in his address information that was already well known. For instance, the end of the Russian war with Turkey had been newsworthy for some months. 'This was an important discovery, indeed!' joked Dan, much to the embarrassed amusement of the House.

He moved on to speak about the state of poverty in Ireland, and criticised the King for saying the distress of the country was merely 'partial'. Was it not true, asked Dan, that 7,000 people in Dublin alone were living on the 'miserable pittance' of three halfpence a day? He spoke about 'the miserable objects of pity' in the three provinces of Leinster, Connacht and Munster. So poor were these 'objects' that rents could only be collected by the threat of execution or 'by the sale of the very blankets with which the unfortunate tenant had been covered'.

After much acclaim and laughter, Dan's maiden speech was hailed as a success. Indeed, Charles Greville corrected himself at once, and praised Dan's efforts in a report the following day: 'O'Connell made his debut, and a successful one, heard with profound attention, his manner good and his arguments attended and replied to.'

Dan spoke regularly during that first week at the Commons, and only five days after the initial address he wrote happily to James Sugrue from his new residence on Maddox Street:

I am fast learning the tone and temper of the House, and in a week or so you will find me a constant speaker.

And so Dan started life as a Member of Parliament. He would go on to become a key figure at Westminster for the next seventeen years.

Immediately, he sought parliamentary reform. This would mean changes in how Parliament was run and, ultimately, look to increase the number of Irish MPs. He also supported universal male suffrage (giving all male adults the right to vote), and he backed the rights of Jewish people. Despite his strong faith, Dan opposed the blasphemy laws, whereby Christians could be jailed or even executed if they criticised God, or denied His existence. He was against military flogging, which allowed soldiers to be whipped violently for stepping out of line.

Significantly, Dan campaigned in Parliament against slavery in all its forms and guises. With his support, both the trade in and ownership of slaves was abolished in the British Empire in 1833. He addressed the issue passionately throughout his political career. Having already 'liberated' the Irish Catholics, he would become, in the words of one black abolitionist, 'a great champion of freedom'. In January 1830, Dan had written a 'letter to the people of Ireland' promising to work on a great many Irish issues, including abolishing tithe payments and repealing the Union.

His new and hectic political career meant that – except on the odd occasion – he had to abandon his law practice. Three homes were now being kept, between various lodgings in London, the house on Merrion Square in Dublin, and Derrynane. More travel also, sometimes for days on end, meant Dan's expenses were rising considerably. Fortunately, his

136

friend P. V. FitzPatrick had already come up with a solution to his financial problems. FitzPatrick set up a fund known as the 'O'Connell tribute'. He arranged for the fund to be collected – like the Catholic rent – at the doors of country chapels. It was to prove an enormous success, with the substantial sum of £13,000 raised annually between 1831 and 1845. The 'tribute' allowed Dan to concentrate fully on the plight of Ireland, and remain as a committed MP.

Only months into Dan's new career, George IV died, in June 1830. The man who had labelled him a 'scoundrel' called out in the night, 'Good God, what is this?', before clasping the hand of his servant to announce, 'My boy, this is death.' A general election soon followed, and Dan was re-elected, this time as an MP for Waterford.

After a brief if well-earned break at Derrynane, he returned to his duties with a public dinner in Killarney that October. The banquet was held to honour the recent revolution in France, and the victory of Catholic Belgium over the tyranny of William I – the Protestant King of the Netherlands.

'As a Catholic I have long watched over the conduct of the Belgians,' said Dan. 'I have admired their honest and persevering patriotism, and felt sympathy in their suffering.'

Indeed, so famous had Dan become internationally that when the Belgians were electing a new king, he had not only been nominated, but he had actually received some votes. The Liberator would later joke that had the nomination come later in his career, he could have challenged the elected King Leopold, or at least 'run the fellow close enough'.

As ever, what Dan was most focused on was the end of the suffering of the Irish. With the hostile Tories in Government, it was at the same Killarney banquet that Dan launched a new campaign to repeal the Union.

137

'The Union should now be agitated in every possible shape,' announced a rejuvenated Dan. It was the first speech on a trail of public meetings and dinners blazed around Munster. The mantra that season was simple: 'AGITATE! AGITATE! AGITATE!'

October was always a month of rest and relaxation, but for Dan in 1830 the spoils of the Kerry Mountains were abandoned for the cause of Ireland and her people. In ten short days, he addressed nine public meetings in places like Waterford, New Ross, Kanturk and Tralee. He had never canvassed so hard, and everywhere he went the peasantry were out cheering 'REPEAL' as his carriage drove by.

When, only a month later, Wellington's Government fell, the Repeal cause was given some hope by the new administration of the more sympathetic Whigs. The new Government tried to win Dan's support immediately, not by supporting Repeal, but by offering him a lucrative job, that of 'Master of the Rolls'. He considered the financial benefits. The new Lord Lieutenant of Ireland, Lord Anglesey, knew Dan's finances were unstable at the best of times, and he tried to convince Dan to take 'the King's shilling'.

In the end, Dan turned down the offer. He would not be bought, and during the 1830s he would resist several more tempting advances from the Whigs. He was in London, after all, to do the business of the Irish people. He always believed there was a better chance of getting what he wanted for Ireland if he refused to cooperate with the Government, and remain a threat.

'If I went into office,' he wrote to a friend, 'I should be their servant – that is their slave. By staying out of office I am to a considerable extent their master.'

Dan might have been new to the workings of Parliament, but after less than a year in the job, he was finding his feet very quickly.

Working for Ireland: 1831–4

While Dan was still in London, Mary sat down to write to him from their house on Merrion Square. It was December 1830 – three decades since they had met – and yet her love for Dan burned as brightly as ever:

My heart overflows with gratitude and pride for being the wife of such a man.

What brought on this latest outpouring was Dan's refusal to accept the Whigs' offer of a Government job.

Thank God you have acted like yourself. Your wife and children have more reason to be proud of you than they ever were.

While refusing office himself, Dan demanded from Lord Lieutenant Anglesey that Catholics get the jobs and positions they now deserved, as their Emancipation had been won. He was told that no such change was likely under the new Government, to which he replied: 'Then it is war between us.'

When both Anglesey and Dan arrived back in Ireland at the end of the year, a game of tit for tat began. The bloody July and August revolutions in France and Belgium had frightened the Government into making sure no such revolt took place in Ireland. Anglesey's objective was now to prevent any meetings that promoted the Repeal of the Union.

139

Dan had only one Repeal organisation, but every time Anglesey's forces attempted to put it down it would re-emerge with a different name. And so, different meetings were prevented, or 'proclaimed', no fewer than four times between 26 December 1830 and 13 January 1831.

Anglesey grew irritated with Dan's constant agitation, and decided to put down 'any association, body, society or party for Repeal, no matter under what title'. When Dan defied this proclamation by inviting 300 of his 'friends' for dinner at Hayes' Tavern, the Lord Lieutenant decided to pounce.

'Things are now come to that pass that the question is whether he or I shall govern Ireland,' Anglesey told his wife.

Within days of the gathering at Hayes' Tavern, Dan was arrested on charges of breaking the ban on public meetings that had been issued by the Lord Lieutenant. Officers Farrell and Irwin arrived at his house to arrest him early on the morning of Tuesday 18 January. They were keen to avoid a scene and asked him to ride in a covered carriage to the police station. Farrell was also suffering from a bad dose of gout.

'I am very sorry for your gout,' Dan declared, 'but since the Lord Lieutenant has chosen to arrest me like a common thief or housebreaker, I think it right the whole city should know it. I must therefore walk!'

Word broke of the Liberator's arrest and soon he was being followed by a bustling throng. Many, like the gaggle of local butchers in tow, were bent on violence. 'No, no!' said Dan. 'That is not my game. I do not want to lose any of your lives. Depend upon it, we shall beat them yet.'

Inside the police station, Dan asked the officers if they could guarantee safety on the streets, should he be held in custody. They agreed they could not, and so Dan guaranteed it himself by posting his own bail, at a hefty cost of £1,000.

Just two months later, on 9 March 1831, Dan made a brilliant speech in favour of a bill for the Reform of Parliament. And, as the Whig Government needed his support for Reform, the charges against him were dropped and the whole affair was soon forgotten about.

This Reform bill came to dominate Dan's year. Although he had fallen out with the Whigs in Ireland, the party's proposed reforms could go some way to helping the country. During the 1831 election campaign, from April to June, nothing was heard of 'Repeal'. Instead, it was all 'Reform'.

'Let no one deceive you and say that I am abandoning my principles of anti-Union,' wrote Dan, in a letter to the people of Ireland. 'Repeal of the Union is the only means by which Irish prosperity and Irish freedom can be secured. But it is only in a reformed Parliament that the question can be properly discussed.'

That year in Parliament was a busy one. Over the seventy-seven days on which Dan attended the House of Commons in 1831, he spoke on no fewer than 283 occasions. Although he was delighted to be elected as an MP for Kerry that year, he was nonetheless bitterly disappointed with the Reform bill that was eventually passed. In theory, Ireland's growing population entitled the country to a hundred more seats in Parliament than the hundred it already had. The Reform bill gave only five more. Ireland's potential electorate, or number of voters, had also been reduced by 174,000 after the 'forty-shillingers' lost their vote in 1829. The new Reform bill got only 4,000 of that huge number back.

Still, of the 105 MPs elected for Ireland in 1832, thirty-nine were supporters of Repeal. Dan's Irish followers in the House of Commons now included what was known as the 'household brigade'. As well as three of his sons – Maurice, Morgan and John – he was supported by two of his sons-in-law and his brother-in-law, W. F. Finn. While Dan was elected for Dublin in 1832, his new six-man 'tail' had been elected for different constituencies.

With Dan's support – along with that of his 'tail' – the Whigs held on to power, but one of their first big actions after the election would have a brutal effect on Irish Catholics. The Coercion Act of 1833 was introduced on 14 February, which allowed the police to put down – with force – any disturbances in the Irish countryside. And not without reason – as the Prime Minister, Charles Grey, had gloomily told the House of Lords, there

had been 242 murders in Ireland in 1832 alone. There had also been 300 attempted murders, and hundreds of cases of assault and arson.

Lord Anglesey had set the bill in motion when he wrote to the Cabinet in January of 1833. His letter claimed the people of Ireland believed the Repeal of the Union was 'within their power to accomplish'. He was letting London know the 'power' he was talking about was violence. The bill banned public gatherings of any kind, or the meetings of any 'dangerous associations in Ireland'. Regular courts could be replaced with harsher military courts. Wrongdoers could be jailed immediately without trial. All meetings to discuss petitions to Parliament were banned. All this added up to a bill that was one of the most brutal ever proposed for Ireland. It was introduced for discussion on 27 February 1833.

In a campaign throughout the spring, Dan argued and debated, pulled the bill apart, and worked to make it a weaker thing, step by step.

'The atrocious attempt to extinguish public liberty with which Ireland is menaced has made me young again,' Dan told his friend Edward Dwyer. 'I feel the vigour of youth in the spring of my hate of ministerial tyranny.'

By the end of March, he had secured many changes to the bill. The new bill, with his many amendments, was made law on 2 April 1833. It was a small victory for Dan over a Whig Government he labelled as 'base, bloody and brutal'.

Many of the disturbances and murders that had prompted the introduction of the Coercion Act were a result of the forced payment of tithes to the Protestant Church of Ireland. The tithe was money paid for the upkeep of the 'Established Church' and it had long been a source of resentment among Catholics. Not just because it was an alien Church, but because its members were associated with all the wrongs ever done to Irish Catholics. So poor were the peasants that many faced starvation if they were to pay the dreaded tithe. But it was the law, and the rectors of parishes saw it as their right to collect the tithes by any means.

A tithe 'proctor', or agent, was sent into a parish to seize the furniture, cow or pig of those unwilling or unable to pay up. This often occurred without violence, but such confiscation was often countered by having no one to buy the stock when it came to auction. Tensions simmered, and death and even massacre soon followed an early period of passive resistance.

For instance, in June 1831, when cattle were seized and put up for sale at Newtownbarry in County Wexford, a riot took place, with police jeered and stones thrown. In the middle of the excitement some of the cattle broke free. This prompted their rightful owners to attempt to take them back. The Yeomanry present were quick to open fire and sprayed the market area with bullets. The peasantry scattered, but fourteen remained – dead in the mud.

Six months later, at Carrickshock in Kilkenny, another bloody incident took place. A local man, James Butler, was hired to issue written warnings

143

to a number of locals who refused to pay tithes to the parish vicar. When Butler and thirty-eight armed constables moved towards the parish, the bells of surrounding Catholic chapels rang out a warning. Suddenly, between two high stone walls along a boreen, the troops and Butler were seized upon by over a thousand men, women and children. Rocks from the walls began to fly as the peasants took out their anger on the tithe collectors. As one youth made a lunge at Butler, he was stabbed and shot dead by the constables. Butler was then struck on the skull by a rock, and dropped dead on the spot. In the riot that followed, eighteen constables were killed by blows from rocks and hurleys, and stab wounds from pikes and scythes. It was the bloodiest incident of the Tithe War.

Dan was called to defend the locals in the case that followed. It was one of the few times he returned to his legal practice after 1830 and, much

like the Doneraile case, he proved he had not lost any of his talents. His defence of a farm labourer named Kennedy was a success against all the odds. A constable who survived the attack was a witness for the prosecution, and his evidence was considered convincing by those present. But Dan turned the case around, and got Kennedy off the hook, when he proved the constable was lying in court, and was thus a perjurer.

Dan felt deeply about the injustice of the tithes to the Church of Ireland. He outright refused to make these payments himself. One night at a London banquet, he told the story of a young girl who had been murdered by soldiers collecting them. His oratory was so powerful that at the end there was hardly a dry eye at the meeting. So moved were the crowd – which included some Members of Parliament – that many came forward afterwards to shake Dan's hand.

Along with his old friend Bishop Doyle, Dan continued to campaign for the complete abolition of tithes, and from June 1833 the Government abandoned the use of soldiers and police to enforce payment. One year later, in June 1834, Dan worked desperately to make vital changes to the tithe laws. The House of Commons accepted his proposals, but his old enemies in the Lords threw them out. It was not until 1838 that the problem was in some way resolved, when tithes became a tax on the landlord's rent. It was then that the Tithe War finally, mercifully, came to a halt.

The aim of the Coercion Act of 1833 was to prevent such occurrences as Newtownbarry and Carrickshock from happening again. When it had passed into law, Dan knew Repeal was out of the question for the time being. He was pushed into arguing for it, however, by a number of supporters, most notably the MP for Cork, Feargus O'Connor. Dan felt that O'Connor and others were merely 'working up their popularity' by pushing for a debate on Repeal in Parliament, when there was no chance of success. Even so, O'Connor had worked up great excitement in Ireland on the issue, with newspaper articles and outdoor meetings.

After much pressure, Dan finally agreed to argue for Repeal at the

House of Commons on 22 April 1834. He spent weeks studying the history of Ireland since the thirteenth century, in a bid to illustrate the wrongs done to her by England. He felt fatigued and overburdened coming up to the debate: 'I never felt half so nervous about anything as I do about my Repeal effort.' He almost despaired: 'It will be my worst. I sink beneath the load.'

But come the hour, come the man. Dan was in fighting form on the morning of the debate: 'The great day has arrived, big with the fate of Cato and Rome.' He left his quarters at Langham Place in brisk fashion, and a troupe of London's Irish emigrants quickly followed him, serenading him across London with shouts and cheers. Suddenly, he received a great clap on the back.

'There you are, Dan O'Connell,' shouted the former boxing champion John Gully, 'going down cool and quiet to your work.'

146

The men were old friends. Dan quickly set himself in the position of a boxer, ready for a bout. 'Yes!' said Dan. 'Tell me Gully, is not that the way to do it?!'

A cheer went up, and Dan was ready to fight his own corner in the House of Commons.

He stood for over five hours arguing for Repeal. He outlined to the House 'all the evils which the English Government have for centuries inflicted upon Ireland'. The speech was pitch-perfect. He showed expertise in the history of Ireland under British rule, emphasising how the country had not prospered 'by or since the Union'. Immediately after the speech, he claimed his words should have been reprinted as a pamphlet, such was their quality.

But Dan knew better than anyone that Repeal in 1834 was not a possibility. While it had the support of thirty-nine Irish MPs, Emancipation had had much more support in Parliament at the height of its campaign in the late 1820s. And while Feargus O'Connor himself also made a spirited pro-Repeal speech in the days that followed, the House was more in the mood for the powerful anti-Repeal speech given by the Protestant politician Emerson Tennent. The motion for Repeal was thus defeated by an overwhelming majority of 523 votes to 38.

One night during the week-long debates, Dan left the House of Commons without his great cloak, and struck out on foot for his residence across the city. The next morning he awoke with a sore throat and headache, and confined himself to the house for the day. With the latest defeat and this small illness, his health and spirits had again been checked. But only momentarily.

The pressure was off from the Repealers at home. He had kept them happy by standing and arguing the case for Ireland. Dan would never join the Whig Government, but at least now he was free to work and compromise with them. With such an immense majority at the House of Commons against Repeal, this was now the solution that promised the most for Ireland.

For the time being at least.

IN THE HOUSE AND ON THE ROAD: 1834-9

O nly months before an autumn fire stormed through Westminster, destroying government buildings, Prime Minister Charles Grey's Whig Government had likewise gone up in smoke. The Government collapse in the summer of 1834 was caused directly by Dan's interference.

The Whigs had wanted Dan's support, and so Richard Wellesley, the new Lord Lieutenant of Ireland, was willing to propose more favourable changes to the brutal Coercion Act of 1833. When Dan met Chief Secretary Edward Littleton in secrecy, he was promised much, and left the meeting in London's Whitehall with high hopes.

Shortly after, while perusing the newspapers, Dan discovered no changes at all would be made to the Act. He was furious. Littleton had promised Dan that he would resign if changes were not made, so when Dan revealed all to a shocked and scandalised House of Commons, Littleton had no other option but to step down. Within days, both Prime Minister Grey and the Chancellor of the Exchequer, Lord Althorp, had also stepped down. It was amid this tumult that Lord Melbourne took over as Whig Prime Minister at 10 Downing Street.

148

His short term in office was marked by the disastrous autumn fire (which, in fact, was started accidentally by two Irish maintenance workers).

At this time, a cholera epidemic was sweeping through Ireland, so Dan made his way from London to Derrynane in August 1834 via Waterford. Dublin was ravaged by the disease, and he for once chose to avoid the capital. During a three-month stay by the shores of the Atlantic, he plotted his next move. Those autumn days at Derrynane had taken on a familiar pattern: Dan would alternate between a day of study and politics at home, and a day rambling through the gorse and bracken, hunting on the hills. When he stopped to take breakfast 'on one of nature's rude imperishable benches', he loved to joke about with the men from the estate.

However, his sport on the mountains never took him too far from current affairs and the news of the day. A post boy would arrive with letters and newspapers, which Dan liked to read aloud for all attentive ears. In autumn 1834 the papers were full of the trials of Poland, where the people were experiencing a famine after a failed harvest. A new statue of the late Prime Minister and 'bad poet' (as Dan had described him) George Canning got some coverage, as did the death of the Queen of Spain. Many pages were dedicated to the 'Burning of Parliament'. *The Freeman's Journal* even carried news of the strange case of 'The Ghost of Saint Giles'. The spook of London turned out to be an Irish emigrant woman whose night-time cries for a lost child had the city in a frenzy. Once the papers were read they were quickly 'flung aside'. These were happy days that allowed Dan to relax and refresh his mind for the more pressing issues that lay ahead.

The humiliating Repeal defeat in the House of Commons in April had already forced Dan to abandon that campaign and focus on a new approach. Even so, he promised his friend FitzPatrick that Repeal was still the priority: 'My conviction on that subject is really unalterable, but for now I will get what I can'.

And so he decided to ally himself with the Whigs. The new strategy would have mutual benefits. In order to oust the new Peel-led Tory

149

Government, which had wrenched back power, the Whigs needed the support of Dan and his 'tail' of Repeal supporters. In return, the Whigs promised improvements for Ireland once their return to Government was secured. In a series of meetings at Lichfield House at the start of 1835, in what became known as 'The Lichfield House Compact', the Whigs committed themselves to abolishing tithes and reforming the administration of Ireland. In return, Dan offered them over sixty votes from Irish MPs and a promise to avoid any topics on which they differed until the Tories had been ousted.

The Compact worked, and Peel's Tory Government resigned in April 1835 after repeated attempts to pass new bills were defeated by the alliance of Dan and the Whigs. Dan was jubilant, and wrote an open letter in the newspapers addressed to 'the people of Ireland':

> A new day begins to shine upon us – a new era opens for Ireland – an Administration is formed, pledged to justice for Ireland. I avow myself the devoted supporter of that Administration.

The Tories were quickly on the attack and Lord Alvanley, in a House of Lords debate, accused the Whigs of receiving Dan's 'dishonourable' but powerful help in regaining power. Alvanley was an old friend of George IV and a trenchant anti-Catholic. He accused the reinstated Prime Minister Melbourne of conspiring with Dan, whose only aim, according to Alvanley, was to ruin the constitution. Two days later, Dan let loose in the House of Commons, labelling Alvanley as nothing more than a 'bloated buffoon' who was 'half idiot, half maniac'.

Alvanley was so disgusted when Dan refused to end the argument with a duel that he attempted to get him kicked out of a Whig social club he frequented, called Brooks'. The club's management, which included Home Secretary Lord Duncannon, refused to expel Dan. They claimed that as the quarrel was personal it was none of the club's business.

Nonetheless, Dan was shunned by many members on his next visit, with some even turning their backs to him. His son Morgan was fuming at such an insult to the family's honour, and the ex-military man decided himself to challenge Alvanley to a duel. In the end, however, and in Dan's absence, the pair managed only to get off three harmless shots between them, in front of a clergyman and a beggarwoman at London's Regent's Park.

However, shortly after Morgan laid down his pistols he was challenged to another duel. This time the offended party was the young politician and writer Benjamin Disraeli. As a young Whig candidate three years earlier, Disraeli had received Dan's backing. Since, however, Disraeli changed his stripes to become a hostile Tory. During the election of 1835 he criticised the Whigs for grasping Dan's 'bloody hand'. Dan quickly answered the insult with one of his most vicious speeches.

'England is degraded,' said Dan, 'in tolerating, or having upon the face of her society a miscreant of his abominable, foul and atrocious nature.'

Dan said Disraeli had the same qualities as the thief beside Jesus on the cross. The thief's name, said Dan, 'must have been Disraeli'.

Incensed, Disraeli answered back in an open letter, addressed 5 May 1835, for the public to see. He first referred to Dan as a beggar for taking the money of Catholics in the form of the Tribute.

'I am not,' said Disraeli, 'one of those public beggars that we see swarming with their boxes in the chapels of your creed. Nor am I in possession of a princely revenue arising from a starving race of fanatical slaves.'

If these words were not obvious enough in their meaning, Disraeli made things even clearer when he wrote to Morgan the next day:

I wished in the open letter to express the utter scorn in which I hold your father's character, and the disgust with which his conduct inspires me ... I shall take every opportunity of holding your father's name up to public contempt, and I fervently pray that you, or someone of his blood, may attempt to avenge the inextinguishable hatred with which I shall pursue his existence.

Morgan refused to deal with a man who was so obviously out of control, and he sent a brief note to Disraeli telling him just that. Despite the end of the affair being reached, Disraeli would maintain his contempt for Dan. It was all of two years later when he finally got to make his first speech as an MP. He hoped to make his mark by attacking Dan and was cheered on by the Tories, including the usually reserved Robert Peel. Dan's supporters did the loudest shouting, however, and Disraeli had to sit down, defeated. 'Though I sit down now,' he shouted across, 'the time will come when you will hear me.'

Not long after the initial dispute, Dan and Morgan set out on a tour of Britain, neatly titled a 'mission to the people of England and Scotland'. Although it lasted only ten days, beginning on 11 September 1835, it took in four major northern cities: Manchester, Newcastle-upon-Tyne, Edinburgh and Glasgow. On tour, one of the main issues brought up by Dan was the corrupt and extravagant power wielded by a paltry few in the House of Lords.

'Liberty is an empty name,' said Dan, 'if any two hundred men, no matter by what titles or denominations styled, can prevent every improvement in the social system and continue every abuse.

It was a popular subject in the region. Many of those who wanted a new system in Parliament – reformers – were based in the north. Indeed, on the first leg of the

tour in Manchester, Dan was overcome by the great welcome he received from over 30,000 people. 'I never was so well received in Ireland,' he told FitzPatrick. Taken aback by the popular emotion of the English, he felt the next step in his career was that of a Cabinet minister, with all 'matters in Ireland officially committed' to him.

He was met with all forms of hospitality along the roads and byways of England, with many people turning out to cheer and shout him on. Even the Dean of York, a brother-in-law of Robert Peel, came up and introduced himself while Dan and Morgan were wandering through the town. The Dean invited the two to dine with him, but was politely declined. Dan was then shown around York Minster, the famous cathedral in the town centre, before heading to the town gardens where many of the townsfolk awaited him. The Dean reappeared with his wife, Peel's sister, and heartily introduced her. Dan was much pleased by all the fuss, and formed a fond opinion of both the people and the town.

After their short respite, Dan and Morgan left York on the afternoon of 13 September and headed north. Travelling with two horses – instead of the usual four – the 56-mile trip to the small village of Rushyford took over seven hours. The lonesome road had Dan thinking of home as he wrote that night from a country inn.

Darling love, how I long to hear from you and all my children! I long to see sweet Sonny again, and his buttercup of a sister.

Eventually Dan's carriage reached Newcastle-on-Tyne. After addressing a gathering of thousands at St Nicholas Square, he was welcomed to a public dinner at the Music Hall where a number of ladies seated in the gallery gave an air of merriment and beauty to the scene. From Newcastle, Dan pushed on, against the rains of September, up towards Scotland. When he reached Edinburgh, a reporter for the *Caledonian Mercury* was there to witness the scene:

The people crowded round his carriage in their eagerness to get a near view of him, and he replied to their salutations with the greatest affability and good humour. On the whole he certainly is a remarkable-looking man. His countenance is striking and expressive, full of animation and intelligence, and when he smiles it is extremely pleasing.

Dan had decked himself out in an extravagant outfit of green overcoat, vest and pantaloons. He topped it all off with a green travelling cap circled with a gold band. He impressed the people of Scotland hugely, both in Edinburgh and, two days later, Glasgow. It was here that he gave one of his many great speeches on the sins of slavery. American slave owners were, he said, no better than 'wolves of the forest' and 'monsters' in human form. 'They boast of their liberty,' said Dan, 'and of their humanity, while they carry the hearts of tigers within them.' He spoke of the slave mothers whose infants were born into shackles. Instead of a blessing, he said, the mother 'feels that in each child she has been visited with a curse'.

Dan tugged at the heartstrings of the Scots, and it was while among them that he famously labelled the Duke of Wellington a 'stunted corporal' and 'the chance victor of Waterloo'. The recent Chief Secretary of Ireland, Henry Hardinge, was just 'a one-armed ruffian', while he called Robert Peel 'the greatest humbugger of the age. As full of cant as any canter who ever canted in this canting world.'

Dan was greeted with 'great laughter and cheering' in Glasgow, as well as in the smaller towns of Falkirk, Greenock, Kilmarnock and Paisley. He even boasted to FitzPatrick that he had become 'exceedingly popular' with the people of northern Britain. Buoyed by his success, he came quickly down to earth on returning to Ireland that autumn, when he became embroiled in controversy.

In November, *The Freeman's Journal* published correspondence between Dan and one Alexander Raphael, off whom Dan was accused – and later cleared – of trying to make money. It was reported that Dan attempted to secure for Raphael a seat in Parliament for County Carlow for a mere £2,000. Raphael won the seat for Carlow, but promptly lost it again after his election was deemed invalid. When he sought to get his money back he was denied it. The whole episode reflected badly on Dan, who longed for a spell in the Kerry countryside, as he had been tied all year to the busy hubbub in England and Dublin.

'I want the calm and quiet of my loved native hills,' he wrote. 'The bracing air, purified as it comes over the world of waters, the cheerful exercise, the majestic scenery of those awful mountains ... the mighty Atlantic, that breaks and foams with impotent rage at the foot of our stupendous cliffs.'

But there was to be little peace of mind for him in 1836, with both professional and personal troubles clouding the year. The affair with Raphael was dragged up again in the House of Commons at the start of February. While Dan was eventually cleared of any wrongdoing, it took a few months to get to that point and his name had been tarnished in the meantime.

Much more troubling was the sharp decline in health of his beloved Mary. She had been poorly the previous autumn, yet despite not much improvement by April 1836 she decided to support Dan on a brief tour of some English industrial towns. The ladies of Nottingham even presented her with a veil for their 'admiration of the domestic support and zealous encouragement which she has always given her husband'. Mary was never one for the limelight and it would prove to be her last excursion with Dan in his professional capacity.

'God help me,' he cried in September 1836, when they had returned to Kerry. 'My ever beloved is in a state of much suffering and is daily losing ground ... I do most potently fear she cannot recover ... I am too weak to do my public duty and this is what she would condemn. But I think I can rally.'

And rally he did, for his son Maurice was also on the verge of death. He was suffering from tuberculosis and had been confined to bed. As Mary was in such a state that she would not notice he was away, Dan set out for Dublin in his carriage. He was determined to find out the best course of action for his son. But he had got only as far as Killarney when, on 31 October, word reached him that Mary had passed away.

She was laid to rest on the small Abbey Island next to Hunting Cap, the other great figure in Dan's life. Dan wrote of Mary shortly after her death that she was 'the most right thinking woman I ever knew'. Indeed she was right, when many others were wrong. Before Dan's Repeal speech and humbling defeat at the Commons in 1834, Mary was, said Dan, 'strongly against my taking part'. Since 1800 she had been like Dan's lighthouse on the shore, and a woman with whom he shared the gift of seven children (and another five who had died in infancy).

Maurice, despite his ill health, continued as MP for Tralee. The feisty Morgan and John were also sitting MPs in 1836. Young Daniel junior was brewing his own stout: 'The very best Irish porter I ever tasted,' said Dan. That venture was doomed, however, because the porter being made by a certain Protestant family by the name of Guinness in Dublin was even better. Ellen, the eldest daughter, was a poet and married to Christopher Fitzsimon, another of Dan's 'tail' at Westminster, while Kate was married to Charles

O'Connell, 'an excellent country gentleman'. The once-doted-on Betsey (Elizabeth) was, in 1836, living in Ros-common with her husband, Nicholas French.

With his wife gone and his children grown, Dan was engulfed in a despair he had never known. To combat it, he resolved to take up the fight for Ireland as never before.

Things in Dublin had been changing, and a new regime at Dublin Castle began to give Ireland a glimmer of hope. Along with a new Lord Lieutenant (Mulgrave) and Chief Secretary (Morpeth), Thomas Drummond had entered office as Under-Secretary in 1835. Although of lower rank than the other two, Drummond's force of character and relentless work dominated the new Whig regime in Ireland. He was a Scotsman who had already worked in Ireland on the first Ordnance Survey of the country. On his journeys throughout the countryside he had seen – and had been appalled by – the incredible poverty and destitution. Now, at Dublin Castle, he was committed to the improvement of Ireland. His time in office would see a great number of Catholics and liberal Protestants appointed to high position. Emancipation was finally bearing fruit at the top levels. A great many of the positions being filled were on Dan's recommendation and from the patronage he was given.

Not only were Catholics being given prestigious jobs, like that of Solicitor General, High Sheriff, Justice of Peace and Registrar of Deeds, they were also entering the police force in large numbers. The long tradition of hiring only Protestants to positions of influence had at last been shattered. The new administration also suppressed the aggressive Protestant Orange Order and assured all landlords that they not only had rights – they also had duties. Drummond insisted it was the neglect of these duties which had Ireland in such a diseased state. When young Princess Victoria became Queen, after the death in 1837 of William IV, the old culture of Establishment bigotry seemed well and truly dead. Until the reign of Victoria, said Dan, 'there never was a sovereign on the British throne sincerely friendly to the people of Ireland'.

With these advances in Dublin and London, Dan decided to give the new regime a chance to prove itself, in what he described as an 'experiment': 'If we shall be deceived, we can fall back on our own resources,' he said.

And so the shout for Repeal was abandoned – for the time being. With the help of Drummond the solutions to many of Ireland's problems were being quickly found. The old tithe system was finally abolished in 1838. A Poor Law came into effect the same year to relieve the most wretched, and Drummond's work in planning a new railway system promised employment and much advancement.

But for all his work with the Whigs, many in Ireland felt that Dan should not have wavered from his goal of Repeal. He was clear about his reasoning, however:

I may be blamed by some for supporting the present Administration instead of looking for Repeal; but in the first place the cry for Repeal would only give increased strength to the vile Orange faction ... In the next place I want to realise as much good for Ireland as I possibly can ... I stand exceedingly well with the present Ministry. They have but little patronage, but that little will be disposed of only to sincere friends of the country. I have, indeed, been of some service to the Government.

Yet many of Dan's supporters did not see things so favourably. The lot of Catholics was improving at the highest levels, but the poor were getting poorer. The population was rising to record levels. The patches of land, on which they had to subsist, were getting smaller and smaller, and the food to feed them becoming more and more scarce. Many felt Dan had abandoned them by working so closely with the traditionally cruel English Government. As a result, the money coming into the O'Connell Tribute fell dramatically, and by the end of the 1830s Dan's hope was again turning to despair.

'I look upon myself in danger of ruin,' he confided to FitzPatrick. 'The country is plainly tired of my claims. I am indeed unhappy ... I do not believe I will long survive the blow from the desertion of me by the country at large. It weighs upon my heart and interferes with my health. All this in the most strict secrecy. At my time of life mental agony is poisonous.'

And yet, even though his popularity was waning, he would not abandon his people. The administration had offered him the highest law position in the land, as Chief Baron. It would have allowed him security and comfort as he headed into old age. But he would not be bought.

'I do not intend to accept any office whilst Ireland is so totally unredressed,' he told FitzPatrick. 'I nail my colours to my country's mast.'

THE MAYOR OF DUBLIN AND THE ROAD TO REPEAL: 1840–2

'You vagabond!' shouted Dan across the Kerry Mountains. 'Have you got no better business than to be abusing my dogs?' He was addressing one of his men – a burly fellow – who had taken to blaming Dan's beagles for losing the scent of a hare. On this particular morning Dan had risen at six o'clock and set about traversing the rocky terrain between Derrynane and Sneem – some 14 miles.

It was the final months of the 1830s. A light sea breeze wafted in off Kenmare Bay, and there was no sound save for the cry of his beagles.

The calm allowed Dan to reflect on his gains and losses, what was done and what still needed to be done. He decided on the next course of action.

'I have done experimenting on the British Parliament,' he told his colleague Thomas Ray. 'I shall now go for the Repeal.'

Dan's alliance with the Whig Government had reaped some rewards, and had been popular with the middle classes. But the popularity he had enjoyed during the Emancipation days, particularly among the poor, had waned long ago. When Under-Secretary Thomas Drummond died from exhaustion on 15 April 1840, a mini-era of cooperation between Dan and Dublin Castle came to an end.

On the same day as Drummond's death, Dan launched his new Repeal campaign at the Corn Exchange on Burgh Quay in Dublin. The new organisation was named the 'National Association of Ireland, for full and prompt Justice or Repeal'. Among its main principles was that it was a movement of complete non-violence, and it was devoted to the monarchy and to religious equality. All religions were welcome to participate in the campaign to abolish the Union of the United Kingdom of Great Britain and Ireland.

Dan's idea of how the Union should be abolished was the same as it had been when William IV was king in 1834: 'We ought to regard Ireland as a limb of the empire – as another and a distinct country, subject to the same King, but having a legislature totally independent of the legislature of Great Britain.'

In keeping with one of the organisation's main principles, the man who chaired proceedings at the Corn Exchange was a Protestant, John O'Neill. Although fewer than fifty men were in attendance, Dan hailed the first meeting of the National Association as a great success. On the brief walk home afterwards, he expressed his opinion to his private secretary and old friend, O'Neill Daunt.

'Yes,' he said, 'I felt that the occasion required a great effort, and I made the effort. This day will hereafter be remembered in the history of Ireland.'

Daunt mentioned the small attendance, but Dan was defiant, and reminded his trusty lieutenant of the first days of the Catholic Association.

'The scanty attendance of this day matters nothing,' said Dan. 'The people remained away because they have not yet found out that I am in earnest. They think I'll drop this agitation yet ... You'll see how they will crowd in to us, as soon as they find out I am seriously determined to go on with it.'

Shortly after this, Dan made it clear exactly how serious he was about the new campaign: 'The Repeal and the Repeal alone is, and must be, the grand basis of all future operations, hit or miss, win or lose.'

He struggled to raise the public's interest, however, and it was not until after the summer elections of 1841 that things began to change. Archbishop McHale of Tuam declared himself in favour of Repeal. He was followed by many of the bishops and most of Connacht's parish priests. The peasantry quickly followed the lead of their clergymen. The Repeal association also changed its name to the more simple 'National Association of Ireland'. Dan looked to enrol people of all classes and creeds into a movement that would copy that of the great Emancipation struggle.

'All I ask of the people is that they should pay individually a farthing a week, a penny a month, a shilling a year, with four weeks thrown in for nothing.'

Repeal 'wardens' were appointed, four in towns and two in country parishes. Their job was to collect these pennies, shillings and farthings, otherwise known as the 'Repeal Rent'. The wardens were controlled by county inspectors, who in turn answered to provincial inspectors. At the top of this vast network stood Dan and a small circle of close confidants. As well as O'Neill Daunt, two journalists were heavily involved – John Gray of *The Freeman's Journal* and Richard Barrett of the *Pilot*. Thomas Ray was the secretary of the new National Association of Ireland, and it was thanks to his talents for organisation that the countrywide network worked so well.

Beside Dan throughout the whole Repeal campaign would be 'Head Pacificator' Tom Steele. Steele was an eccentric Protestant from County Clare who devoted his life to Dan. He had been his loyal comrade during the Clare election of 1828 and now, well over a decade later, he was still in tow. Decked out in semi-military dress, with a peaked cap, blue coat, white trousers and Wellington boots, Steele followed Dan everywhere. Indeed, as 'Pacificator' he was sent out to keep the peace and would arrive at rural trouble spots in a coach draped in 'mourning cloth'. With furious and theatrical expression, spittle spewing from his toothless mouth, he would shout down the wrongdoers. It was said that 'Honest Tom', as he was sometimes called, was more potent than the police at putting down agrarian crime.

It was during these days that Ireland was granted the final great measure that resulted from Dan's alliance with the Whig Government. The Municipal Reform Act threw the halls of local power open to Catholics, and Dan decided to act on this at once by standing as a candidate for Lord Mayor of Dublin. His election on 1 November 1841 had been a foregone conclusion, with three-quarters of the newly elected members of Dublin Corporation who would be voting either supporters of Repeal or at least Whigs. When Dan won, it was the first time in 150 years that a Catholic had held the prestigious position of Dublin's Lord Mayor. As Lord Mayor, he stated his intentions immediately: of being civil and working for people of all persuasions.

'I pledge myself to this,' he announced on election night, 'that in my capacity as Lord Mayor no one shall be able to discover from my conduct what is my religion, or of what shade are the politics I hold.'

That evening he made his way to a balcony of the Corporation building on William Street to address the multitudes gathered outside. He revelled in his new wine-red robes, and he asked the boys in the crowd if his hat suited him. 'Shure you're the finest Lord Mayor we ever saw,' came a cry from the crowd below.

After all the celebration on the night, Dan took his new post seriously and looked upon it as a way to show the authorities what would happen if the Irish were allowed to govern themselves independently as a limb of the Empire. That Empire was now under the control of Dan's old foe

Robert Peel, who became Prime Minister after the Whigs had been defeated in the August election. Other adversaries of Dan's had joined Peel in the new Tory Cabinet, such as Wellington and Lord Stanley.

With the Whigs out of Government and the money from the O'Connell Tribute reducing still further, Dan relied more and more on the ceaseless work of his financial manager, FitzPatrick, in raising the new Repeal Rent. When the British peer Lord Shrewsbury criticised Dan for accepting the pennies of the poor, Dan spoke about all he had given up during his life in his pursuit of justice for the Irish people:

My claim is this. For more than twenty years before the Emancipation the burden of the cause was thrown upon me – I had to arrange the meetings – to prepare the resolutions – to furnish replies to the correspondence – to rouse the torpid – to animate the lukewarm – to control the violent ... Who shall repay me for the lost opportunities of acquiring professional celebrity, or for the wealth such distinctions would ensure? I assert that no man ever made greater sacrifices for what he deemed the cause of his country than I have done. I care not how I may be ridiculed or maligned. I feel the proud consciousness that no public man has made more, or greater, or more ready sacrifices.

After a year in the Lord Mayor's office, which included a visit to Buckingham Palace to meet Queen Victoria, Dan retreated to the wilds of Derrynane to rejuvenate and to prepare the ground for 1843. He would christen it 'The Repeal Year'. Thomas Ray, O'Neill Daunt and Dan's son John were sent out around the country to pave the way for a new, vigorous movement. John, for instance, travelled around Connacht and held meetings in Carrick-on-Shannon, Roscommon, Castlebar and Carracastle, all the while receiving assistance from the Archbishop of Tuam. These missions to rural Ireland reignited the popularity Dan would enjoy throughout 1843.

Also vital was the publication of *The Nation,* a new newspaper for the Repeal movement. It was set up by a group of young men – Charles Gavan Duffy, John Blake Dillon and Thomas Davis. Whereas Dan's goals were mainly political, the aim of *The Nation* was to promote and revive Irish culture. It printed poems and ballads, promoted the Irish language, and looked to resurrect the forgotten legends of Irish history. Within months of its foundation *The Nation* became the most widely circulated and read paper in Ireland.

All these factors contributed to the blossoming of Repeal, and by the start of 1843 Dan was the leader of a movement that would become as widespread, powerful and well organised as the one that had won Emancipation.

THE REPEAL YEAR: 1843

On 1 January 1843 Dan sat at his desk at Derrynane and wrote a letter to the Irish people. It would appear in the newspapers six days later, and it began by quoting his favourite line from Byron:

'Hereditary bondsmen! know ye not
Who would be free themselves must strike the blow?'

In this open letter he again outlined all the ills done to Ireland by her closest neighbour. He also announced that from that day forward, the next twelve months were to be the Repeal Year. At the end of February his address to Dublin Corporation proved the rallying cry that set events in train. He went on to explain his plan to the National Association of Ireland. By travelling around the country on a great tour he would whip up excitement for Repeal at enormous meetings held every Sunday, as well as on Church holidays. The tour would show the Government in London, by way of newspaper reports, the vast number of people who wanted Repeal. It would also show that the movement was peaceful; that neither Dan nor the Irish people wanted trouble. And yet, with the support of thousands, the movement would pose a very real threat.

His first goal was to get three million people enrolled in the National Association of Ireland by the start of August. Then, each district would nominate people to represent it in Dublin at the end of the year. This body would be called the Council of Three Hundred, and it would plan a bill to Repeal the Union.

The first meeting of Dan's great tour was held at Trim in County Meath on Sunday 19 March 1843. It was, according to one reporter, 'magnificent

167

beyond description'. While fog had shrouded the country since dawn, it lifted before noon and by 2 p.m. over 30,000 people had gathered in the town centre under a bright sky.

Dan and Tom Steele had arrived the previous day. After a celebratory journey through the countryside from Dublin they were greeted in the town by triumphal arches and banners of all descriptions. When Dan finally took his stance on a timber platform, to rapturous cheers, it was to be the first of thirty-one outdoor meetings he would address that year. While there were many more meetings he found impossible to attend, his own travels in 1843 covered some 5,000 miles of Irish roads and trails. It was in County Meath, however, that he began his year of agitation and stirring oratory.

'Are you slaves?' he called to the people of Trim. 'And are you content to be slaves? I shall either be in my grave or a freeman ... for I am tired of remaining under submission to others.'

He started as he meant to go on, and to loud cheers he told the assembled masses he would 'never relax in the battle' until victory was his.

This first meeting received enormous coverage in the press, and Repeal fever swept the country. In May alone there were some seven outdoor rallies the length and breadth of Ireland. The term 'monster meeting' was coined by *The Times* of London as an insult to the Irish people. Dan, however, was happy with the term as it gave the events a sense of danger.

Whatever danger Dan wanted the Government to feel, he was also careful to work within the confines of the law. He demanded that the meetings be peaceful, no matter how large the crowds. He felt the huge attendances alone would demonstrate to Peel and his Cabinet exactly what the vast majority of Irish people wanted. Peel would not listen to, look at, or hear of any alternative to Ireland staying under the Union, however. In an attempt to calm the authorities in Dublin Castle, who urged London to clamp down on the rallies, he stood in the House of Commons on 9 May and addressed the issue. He told the Speaker, Mr

Shaw-Lefevre, that he did not favour any kind of war, 'above all, civil war'.

'Yet there is no alternative,' he declared, 'which I do not think preferable to the dismemberment of this great Empire.'

Two weeks later, Dan stood before an immense congregation of close to 100,000 people at Longford and hurled a defiant cry. If the Government attacked them, he said, 'who will be the coward? We will put them in the wrong, and if they attack us then in your name I set them at defiance.'

The Nation was printing every word of these great speeches. It was also publishing the speeches from the banquets that were held in their aftermath. The paper was being read in reading rooms, inns and cabins throughout rural Ireland. As with the struggle for Emancipation before

170

it, the Repeal movement was now coming to the people. With their pennies, shillings and farthings, they were members of the National Association of Ireland, and felt as much a part of the movement as Dan himself. The day a monster meeting would come to their own district was now awaited with the greatest excitement.

Most important to the organising of the meetings was the Catholic clergy. As early as 1840, a great many of Ireland's bishops had declared their support for Dan and the Repeal movement. This was vital, as the National Association of Ireland relied on the parish priests to organise at local level. The priests would nominate good parishioners as Repeal wardens for the district. They would also oversee local Repeal meetings, as well as reading rooms set up to discuss the cause. If a monster meeting was to take place in a locality it was the parish priest who did most of the organising.

In Kells, County Meath, for instance, Fr McEvoy was vital. When a Repeal organiser went to the town to set events in motion, he stayed in the parochial house overnight. Later, Fr McEvoy selected the Repeal wardens for the district, and when Dan came to address a meeting of over 100,000 people, it was Fr McEvoy who was the chief organiser. The priests would also provide accommodation for the other main speakers at the Repeal meetings, and a large number of clergy would appear on stage with Dan and his Repealers, either at the outdoor meeting during the day or at the banquet held later in the evening. On these occasions a toast was usually drunk to the Catholic clergy of Ireland. The movement welcomed Protestants, however, and prided itself on being non-sectarian. Still, they were in the minority and Repeal was mainly a Catholic movement.

To Dan's delight, at some forty monster meetings throughout the year not a single troublesome incident took place. Central to this was the temperance movement begun by Fr Theobald Mathew in the late 1830s. In 1840, Dan, who was never a big drinker himself, took the pledge to abstain completely from alcohol, and by 1842 some five million people had followed his lead. The temperance movement was one of the main

171

reasons why Dan pushed ahead with the Repeal year in the first place. With over 60 per cent of the population pledged against alcohol, the chance of trouble on tour was much smaller.

At the Roscommon rally in August, Dan doubled his efforts in a bid to keep the people away from alcohol. 'Teetotalism is one of our greatest means of success,' he said. 'I have made a rule that no man who breaks the temperance pledge shall be allowed to become a Repealer ... I pronounce that the first precursor of freedom to Ireland is teetotalism, and I believe that Father Mathew was sent by God to bless Ireland with virtue.'

Even without drink, festivities followed Dan wherever he went. On a few occasions, like the meetings held at Tara Hill in County Meath and Mullaghmast in County Kildare, venues were picked for their historical significance. For the most part, though, venues were picked for their location, to attract as many people as possible. The great July meeting at Tullamore in Ireland's centre had people filing in from the surrounding districts for much of the day before. All night long there was bustle in the streets as would be seen on a market day. By the early morning of Sunday 16 July 1843 the town was effectively impassable, such were the crowds. Temperance bands from Roscrea, Athlone, Kilbeggan and Birr led their townsfolk up the street, to the cheers of those already in attendance.

Dan, his son Daniel junior and Tom Steele arrived in a horse-drawn carriage on the Saturday and stayed with Fr O'Rafferty in his mansion. After Dan had gone to Mass on Sunday morning, he proceeded up through the town to a great podium erected at Market Square. There, he promised 150,000 people their own Parliament in Dublin within twelve months. The response from the crowd was loud, continuous cheering.

Such displays of devotion were everywhere. At the Repeal meeting in Ennis the air was given a delightful scent after women and children carried in trees and evergreens from the surrounding countryside. The trees were planted along the streets, while the evergreens were used to decorate the town's houses. The fresh smell was even more agreeable given the heat of the day. Evergreens, laurels, small trees and bushes were used everywhere to adorn meeting places. As well as looking and smelling nice, they cost nothing and could be used to decorate anything – from streets to houses, from stages and triumphal arches to people. Green plants were also symbols of Ireland, and most had to be stolen off the lands and demesnes of the wealthy landlords. The twigs, branches and bushes became like trophies won from the brutal oppressor.

As the year went on and the monster meetings grew in size, the organisers became worried that stealing more and more greenery would lead to violence. Repeal leaders like Steele urged the people not to take so much as a twig, or anything else that could be interpreted by the Protestant Ascendancy as theft. It was in Ennis that Dan promised those peasants who were ripping up their landlords' foliage that victory would soon be theirs:

'Clare is speaking out again ... I am addressing twice as many as ever congregated on the subject of Emancipation. I told you at the time that Emancipation would be useful, principally to the high and rich classes, but the Repeal of the Union will be useful to the poor and humble, to the working classes and the industrial classes.'

The assembly in Ennis was recorded at well over 200,000, but the most striking of all the monster meetings was held on the Hill of Tara on 15 August, the Feast of the Assumption. The reporter from *The Freeman's Journal* estimated there could not have been fewer than half a million people on the historic hill and its surrounds. 'In the history of Ireland,' he wrote the next day, 'and perhaps that of Europe, there is no record of a meeting like that which was witnessed yesterday.' From everywhere the people came. There wasn't a hackney carriage to be found in Dublin – they had all descended on Tara.

Forty-two marching bands enlivened the roads of Meath as representatives from all the districts of Ireland came together. Westmeath, Kildare and Louth were represented. Cavan and Monaghan sent their thousands. There were temperance bands from Longford and Queen's

County (now Laois). The peasants of Tipperary and Wexford had spent days on the road to reach the historic site. Among all these thousands were hundreds of emigrant Repealers from Liverpool, and a priest from Niagara Falls. In the early morning, the fields for miles around were filled with vehicles – carriages and gigs of all description. The sky was just cloudy enough so it was not too hot, and a pleasing and subdued light was cast over the lovely landscape.

Masses were said from 9 a.m. until noon at six altars scattered around the great expanse. One priest preached a sermon on temperance. Raising his hands to the sky, he invoked the blessing of heaven on the thousands and their Liberator. It was, said O'Neill Daunt, 'a sublime spectacle, unsurpassed in the history of the world'. In the middle of this swarm Dan's carriage trundled slowly towards the summit of the hill. It took two hours to travel one mile, even with a mounted escort of 10,000 horsemen. A short distance from the great ringfort, the Fort of the Kings, stood the Liberator's platform. The bishops of Meath and Derry, along with thirty-five priests, welcomed Dan as he arrived to deafening cheers at half past one in the afternoon.

Dan's son John would later say that that day on the Hill of Tara was his father's 'crowning day'. The spectacle would never be matched, and it would leave a lifelong impression on all who were there. What left an impression on the authorities was the fact that it was so trouble-free. What made it so was the use of the 'O'Connell Police'. These were Repeal wardens who had taken Fr Mathew's pledge. These men had the responsibility of keeping the peace at all meetings. As there was virtually no drinking at any of the demonstrations their task was made all the easier.

And yet, in all of Dan's monster meeting speeches he made sure to use the most violent language. He would work the crowd to a frenzy with graphic tales from Irish history. At Mullaghmast in County Kildare, for instance, he spoke of 100 Irish chieftains who had been massacred on the very spot by the English in the 1500s. The men in the audience, reported an English visitor, 'yelled and danced with rage; the women screamed and

Major Repeal Meetings of 1843

clapped their hands. The vast multitude – I believe there were really 100,000 present – moved and moaned like a wild beast in agony.'

Dan knew how to win people's devotion to the cause. In Mallow in County Cork, too, he played on their emotions. The army had congregated outside the town and were ready to squash the meeting. Dan had told the journalists to take down every word he spoke. Trouble was brewing and the place was full of the most frightening rumour when 'Pacificator' Steele told one writer that battle was next: 'Our next move may be to take to the field.'

It was all a trick. Far from fighting the army, Dan praised them to the hilt, saying they were 'the bravest in all the world'. Once the threat was out of the way, he retreated to the banquet in Mallow town where he hurled defiance at Ireland's English masters.

'The time is come when we must be doing,' he shouted. 'Gentlemen, you may soon learn the alternative, to live as slaves, or die as freemen ... In the midst of peace and tranquillity they are covering our land with troops.'

When dinner arrived a singer took the stage and began singing an Irish ballad:

Oh where's the slave so lowly,
Condemned to chains unholy...

Dan sat in silence. Then he burst from his seat. 'I am not that slave!' he yelled, to the shock and fright of the crowd. Then, all in the hall began to copy his words in a defiant chant: 'We are not those slaves! We are not those slaves!'

It was a brilliant piece of theatre from the Liberator. He had set the whole episode in motion, along with the connivance of the singer. The night would become legend, as his words and the chants of the crowd became known to all as the 'Mallow Defiance'.

* * *

For months Peel had wanted to put down Dan's Repeal agitation but couldn't. Within the confines of the law Dan had the right to lead a peaceful agitation, and that was exactly what he was doing. There had not been the slightest trouble at any of the meetings. Indeed, the Lord Chancellor, Edward Sugden, wrote to Peel in May stating as much: 'The peaceable demeanour of the movement is one of the most alarming symptoms.' In any case, the Anti-Corn Law League was carrying out the same kind of agitation in England. If Peel put down one, he would have to put down the other.

The trouble for Peel was that Dan was becoming an all too powerful figure. That was reflected not only in the increasing numbers attending monster meetings (from 30,000 at Trim to 500,000 at Tara), but also in the vast amount of money the National Association of Ireland was receiving in donations. For example, the Repeal Rent had jumped from £360 per week in March to £2,000 per week in May. At Mullaghmast Dan was even presented with a kind of crown. It was a green velvet cap with a rim of gold shamrock. Government spies in the crowd reported that Dan received the crown and placed it on his head – like a king. All of this, and the fact that Dan's alternative government – the Council of Three Hundred – was to gather in December, made the Government determined to act.

The final monster meeting of 1843 was set for Clontarf on the outskirts of Dublin on 8 October. The Liberator's platform would be pitched on Conquer Hill, where the Irish hero Brian Boru died in 1014 while defeating the Viking invaders. Clontarf would be the greatest of all the meetings, a demonstration in size and pageantry to surpass even the Hill of Tara. The people of Dublin would come, and so too the country dwellers. Steamers were set to sail from Scotland and England with thousands of Irish emigrants ready to shout 'Repeal!'

Throughout September the Government was getting ready for a showdown. Troops were sent from Britain to strengthen the Irish garrisons. Ammunition was accumulated. Provisions, food and equipment were packed into Irish depots. Lines of warships sailed into Irish waters. Other detachments waited at port towns in the west and north of England, ready to be deployed. The Home Secretary, James Graham, decided to supress the Council of Three Hundred by force if Dan brought it into being. The Tory Cabinet considered sending Wellington (the victor at Waterloo) to take charge of the military arrangements.

The Government needed a reason to act and it finally got one when advertisements for the Clontarf meeting appeared that contained threatening language. The term 'Repeal Cavalry' did the damage. By describing the planned peaceful, horse-mounted parade from Dublin city centre as a cavalry, the writers had made a massive mistake. Dan publicly dismissed the advertisements as soon as he read them, but it was too late. Dark rumours circulated around the capital on Friday 6 October, but it was not until half past three on Saturday afternoon that the pro-clamation banning the Clontarf meeting was issued from Dublin Castle.

A messenger dashed hotfoot down Dame Street and burst through the doors of the Corn Exchange, where Dan and his National Association of Ireland were meeting. Dan quickly cast his eyes over the proclamation and knew a decision had to be made quickly. The meeting was set for the next day and already the masses were filling the country roads on their way to the capital. Instantly and without hesitation, he accepted the banning of Clontarf. He called on Thomas Ray and dictated an address of explanation to the Irish people. Within minutes this 'counter proclamation' was on its way to the printing presses. Members of the National Association of Ireland set out on horseback to each of the main roads leading to Dublin to turn back the droves of supporters.

Why? As Dan had said only a few months earlier at Skibbereen, 'One living Repealer is worth a churchyard full of dead ones'. No matter how intemperate his language at places like Mallow, the real Dan hated violence. When push came to shove, he would never allow it. In any case, a strict gun law had been brought into Ireland earlier in the year, which meant none of the people on their way to Dublin were armed. If trouble kicked off, he said later, it would have ended 'in the slaughter of the people'.

By Sunday morning, 8 October, thanks to the brilliant management and organisation of the National Association of Ireland, there was scarcely a soul still heading towards Dublin. Tom Steele wandered the grounds in Clontarf, a green laurel bough (the emblem of peace) in his hand. 'Home with ye now,' he called out to a near-empty field. 'Home with ye.'

Even if the Government had abandoned the rule of law by threatening massacre on a peaceful demonstration, the event had provided the Repeal Year with a dramatic ending. It ensured the Association stayed in the spotlight and accumulated even more funds for its 'Repeal Rent'.

But Dan had received a blow. His defiant and violent talk during the year had been exposed, because for him freedom was to be attained not by the flowing of blood but always by peaceful means. His methods would soon cause a split with the more radical young men from *The Nation*. They would become known as 'Young Ireland'.

For now, Dan had to accept defeat. Only days after Clontarf he was arrested along with his son John, Thomas Ray and Tom Steele. Gavan Duffy of *The Nation* was also detained, as were the editors Gray and

Barrett of *The Freeman's Journal* and the *Pilot*. At first Dan was flustered and upset. As he sat in his cell he imagined a grisly death on the gallows as he pondered the hangings of the 1798 Rebellion. But the charge that followed was not for high treason, as he had imagined, but for the less serious offence of 'seditious conspiracy'.

Dan perked up on hearing the charge. 'I do not think two years' imprisonment would kill me,' he remarked to John. 'I should keep constantly walking about and take a bath every day.'

Peel and Dublin Castle were so determined to find Dan and company guilty that the first jury called up were all Protestants. This was obviously unfair and as a result Dan succeeded in postponing the trial until the following January. In the meantime, he and his small band of followers were released on bail.

Off he struck for his native Kerry. Away from the storm and tumult of the year, he was at once calmed by the reassuring, peaceful voices of sea, sky and mountain. He walked for miles that winter, edging along the wild Atlantic on Coomakista Hill. He bounded through gorse and heather with his loyal beagles at his feet.

But the year had taken its toll. Dan's speed of step and of mind was fading gradually. Yet, as the New Year and his trial fast approached, he assured FitzPatrick all was well: 'I already feel the immense benefit of my native air … I am regaining strength and vigour to endure whatever my sentence may be.'

18

Changing Times: 1844-5

an's trial for 'seditious conspiracy' began on 15 January 1844, but a guilty verdict was a foregone conclusion. There was a longlist of forty-eight possible jurors, from which twelve had to be chosen. The authorities immediately dismissed all eleven Catholics on the longlist, leaving only Protestants. Dan and the other 'traversers' (as they became known) would therefore be facing a jury brought together unfairly, no matter who was picked.

The 'Irish State Trials' were a huge affair, and took up acres of newspaper space. They began – predictably enough for Dan – with massive street crowds and fanfare. Dan made his way through the bustle in the Lord Mayor's carriage, accompanied by the current Lord Mayor, Timothy O'Brien.

Dan's co-conspirators were represented in court by the great and the good from the Irish legal circuit. Dan, on the other hand, defended himself, in full regalia of robes and wig. The prosecution for the Crown was led by the Attorney General, T. B. C. Smith, a man so angry and sour in disposition that Dan liked to call him 'the vinegar cruet on two legs'.

After many days of monotony, filled with tedious speeches and opening argument, the trial proper got under way. Dan began by asserting to Judge Perrin that he was in court not to defend himself, but rather to defend the people of Ireland: 'My client is Ireland,' he declared, 'and I stand here the advocate of the rights, and liberties, and constitutional privileges of that people.'

Dan admitted he had been harsh on certain individuals (like Peel and Wellington) during his monster meeting speeches, but he told the court that all else spoken could be justified and defended. He told the judges and jury that he would never make a revolution with blood. 'I would make it with public opinion, and I would put a little Irish spirit in it.'

Many who read the address later thought it was one of Dan's greatest on the blight of English rule in Ireland. But the voice that delivered it was failing. Dan was by now in obvious physical decline. One lawyer present at the trials said solemnly that 'the old fervour had departed, the old mastery was no more'. In spite of this, Dan reminded all present that there had been no secrecy, or 'conspiracy', in the way he had conducted himself during the Repeal Year. In fact, he said, everything had been conducted in the 'open day'.

The massive show of support for Dan and Repeal had been an affront to the Government, however, and the price was going to be paid. The spokesman for the jury, the foreman, came forward with the expected verdicts on Monday morning, 12 February 1844. The courthouse had been abuzz long before 9 a.m., and at five minutes to the hour Dan stepped into the chamber. The judges, Crampton and Burton, took their seats upon the bench shortly after. A hush descended as Crampton began proceedings. It had been a long weekend, with much confusion as to who was to be charged, and with what. Crampton thus outlined the nuts and bolts of the case that had been put to the jury. When all was settled, the gavel came down. A verdict of guilty was announced for Dan and his fellow defendants. They would face all the rigours of the law.

But not just yet. The sentencing was postponed. In the meantime, Dan struck for London, where a week-long debate on the state of Ireland was taking place in the House of Commons. On 15 February, Westminster and its surrounds were a hubbub of noise and excitement. The throngs were looking forward to getting a glimpse of the famous Dan. When a grand horse and carriage was seen meandering down Parliament Street, applause rang out. But inside was Robert Peel. According to the man himself, he had 'been mistaken by the great majority for O'Connell'.

Later that day, in the House of Commons, a liberal MP from Belfast, D. R. Ross, was making a speech in praise of the Liberator. Suddenly, and almost on cue, Dan made a spectacular entrance. The opposition benches all hailed him with fervent cheers, while the Government members mustered up some sneering cries. There had been much boasting by the Government about the victory at his trial in Dublin. It was on this subject that D. R. Ross interrupted the babble of the members: 'Let the House judge by the reception which the *head conspirator* has just met, whether there be much cause for triumph. You may put that man in jail, but what will you gain?'

A public banquet was later held in Dan's honour at Covent Garden Theatre, with up to a thousand people present. Wine glasses were raised to the health of the Liberator. Dan penned a letter to FitzPatrick on the fine treatment he was receiving. 'I certainly did not expect anything half so generous or so kind,' he noted.

Alas, for all the good humour of his English support, Dan's main concern was the decision of Government. Not long after arriving back in Dublin it was time for him to return to court. His sentencing was to be heard on Thursday 30 May. Such was Dan's prestige, he was received inside the court with the grace afforded only to the judges. Many barristers stood up, while the chamber echoed with applause.

The judges present – Crampton, Burton and Perrin – were divided on what sentence Dan should receive. In the end, twelve months' imprisonment was agreed upon. The rest of the accused, including young John O'Connell, were handed lesser sentences of nine months apiece.

Burton had once been a colleague of Dan's on the Munster circuit. After passing the sentence, the old judge hid his hands in his face and wept.

Dark clouds drifted in over the city and, oddly for the time of year, thick snow began to fall. The new prisoners were held in the sheriff's room of the courthouse, while carriages gathered at the rear yard to bring them to Richmond Prison. Shortly after 4 p.m. the cavalcade began its trudge through the city, where thousands of well-wishers had congregated. The crowds remained restrained and silent, following Dan's strictest orders. 'Obey my advice,' he had warned. 'NO RIOT. NO TUMULT. NO BLOW. NO VIOLENCE. Keep the peace for six months ... and you shall have the Parliament at College Green again.'

For all his promises, there was little Dan could do from the confines of jail. Yet he was no ordinary convict. The governor of Richmond Prison, for instance, welcomed him like an old friend. Once inside, he was greeted by his two daughters, Ellen and Betsey. Their presence and support was just one of the many privileges Dan was granted. He and his fellow prisoners, along with their families, were allowed to reside at the governor's lodgings. The place soon resembled a pleasant country house. Each day, fresh venison, game, fish and fruit were sent in as gifts. The living quarters were furnished with plenty of means for study or amusement. A spacious canvas pavilion (titled 'The Rath of Mullaghmast') was erected on the grounds so prisoners, family and guests could dine together. A gymnasium was also provided – though Dan never set foot there. 'Seven times round the jail garden is a mile,' he said. 'I walk it three times a day.'

After two months of prison life, Dan assured Betsey that he was in 'excellent health and spirits'. But the world outside was not in good spirits over Dan's continued imprisonment. He received letters of goodwill from clergy across Europe, including Germany and England. The Catholic bishops of Ireland met and drew up a prayer to be said at every Mass throughout the land. The prayer asked God for Dan's quick release 'for the guidance and protection of his people'. Even the English writer William Makepeace Thackeray, who was no friend to him or Irish Catholics, declared Dan's achievements made him 'THE GREATEST MAN IN THE EMPIRE'.

The National Association of Ireland made an appeal to the House of Lords against the guilty verdict. Not only was the verdict wrong, they stated, but so too was the picking of an all-Protestant jury. Dan feared the authorities would not listen. So effective were the arguments put forward, however, that on 4 September the appeal was heard. At first there was a split decision. Out of five judges, two were in favour of overturning the convictions and two were against. The deciding voice was that of Judge Denman. He voted in favour of the appeal, saying the use of an all-Protestant jury was a 'mockery'.

It was the news all Ireland was waiting for. The first to hear were those lining the quays of Kingstown (now Dún Laoghaire). As evening closed in on 5 September, the packet ship *Medusa* was spotted in the distance. An attorney for the accused, Mr William Ford, was on deck. He waited to get close enough to shore before shouting: 'O'Connell is free!'

A scream of joy went up among the crowd, and wild celebrations followed as a train bearing the message with victory flags chugged its way into Westland Row station. There, horsemen were waiting to race out to Richmond Prison. Each man wanted to be the first to bring the splendid news. A young messenger, Edmond O'Haggarty, won the race and cried out on arrival, 'I'm first, you're free, Liberator, I'm first!'

But Dan was having none of it. 'Bah! It isn't true,' he muttered. 'It can't be true.' He was reassured that it was by his attorney Mr Ford, however, when he arrived white-faced, with tears in his eyes and puffing from his exertions. They shook hands, embraced and wept.

The following day, the prison gates were flung open to allow *in* thousands of well-wishers. Men, women and children lined up in the prison garden to shake the hand of Dan, who stood at the bottom of a little mound, known to all as 'Tara Hill'. After an evening meal, the 'traversers' left the grounds of the prison; Dan made the trek to his Merrion Square house on foot, where he spent the first night of freedom.

In keeping with the drama that typically followed Dan about, it was arranged that all the prisoners should return to Richmond Prison the next morning for a formal, triumphant release. After a night when Ireland from north to south was alight with bonfires, Dan rose early and quietly made his way across south Dublin, until he reached the prison chapel. There he concluded his nine-day novena, before joining the other martyrs for breakfast. Ahead of their departure, Dan arranged for the release of forty-two prisoners of good character. Fines they had been unable to pay were met with funds from the National Association of Ireland.

On this note of generosity and good spirit, Dan emerged from the gates of Richmond Prison. He was led by the hand by William Smith O'Brien MP, to a triumphal chariot made especially for the occasion. Dan, in great cloak and Mullaghmast 'crown', stood regally on the top of its three tiers. Beneath him, an old harper with a long beard played national airs. On the carriage floor were Dan's grandchildren, dressed in green velvet tunics and white-feathered caps.

Before and below Dan stood hundreds of thousands of supporters. The Liberator's chariot led the way, followed by open carriages housing the other 'traversers'. The procession of horses, carriages and marchers stretched back some 6 miles and took hours to travel the short distance into the city. Ships on the river flew colourful bunting of celebration all the way from their decks to their top spar.

When Dan's commanding chariot of purple velvet and gold reached the Parliament House in College Green it creaked to a sudden halt. He remained silent, looking into the eyes of the people. It was here in College Green the Liberator hoped to seat the Irish Parliament once more, after he had shattered the Union. He removed his 'crown', raised his right hand and pointed to the great building. A deafening cheer filled the air. Dan repeated the gesture. Again and again. Each time, the sky was filled with shouts so loud they resembled the howl of the ocean.

Then, with a lurch, the chariot trundled on. It was one of the greatest days the city had seen. The cheering continued long into the evening. On his balcony in Merrion Square, Dan reassured the multitudes below that everything would be done to win the coveted Repeal: 'This is a great day for Ireland. A day of justice ... Yes; I am glad that I was permitted to suffer for Ireland. My course is a course of morality and peace. We have won much by it, and by it we will achieve yet more.'

One week later, at Mass in Dublin, Dan and the traversers received the blessing of Fr John Miley. The reverend father said that it was only by the intervention of the Blessed Virgin Mary the prisoners had been released. Such was the hype and enthusiasm which greeted Dan on the outside.

Yet, despite Dan's promise from his Merrion Square balcony, there was much public doubt as to what the next move would be, and whether he would resume the quest for Repeal with the same gusto as before his imprisonment. At a meeting of the National Association of Ireland in the days soon after his release, no answer to that question was found. Instead, the meeting was more an occasion of celebration and joy for Dan and his supporters.

The Association's new premises at Conciliation Hall was packed to capacity, and many were turned away. Dan received the same great cheering and ovations as ever. And yet there was a slight gloom evident among the crowd. Dan had never seemed so fragile. He had always appeared tall and alert, but now there was a limp in his step and unsteadiness in his countenance. His keen blue eyes looked tired and dull. He was getting old, and his imprisonment had not helped matters. It became evident to all in Conciliation Hall that his fighting spirit was in decline, his energy for agitation sapping. Indeed, a melancholy spread quickly among his followers.

That winter, 1844, Dan retreated to Derrynane to seek solace with his beloved beagles. While he was away, serious unrest began to emerge

(*L–r*): Thomas Davis, Charles Gavan Duffy and John Blake Dillon

among members of the National Association of Ireland. The Young Ireland faction had organised much of Dan's Repeal movement of the previous year. They had also reported and promoted the cause in *The Nation*. Now Charles Gavan Duffy (who had been in jail with Dan), John Blake Dillon and Thomas Davis were becoming baffled and annoyed with what appeared to be Dan's increasing disinterest in Repeal. Already, from the seclusion of Derrynane, Dan had been corresponding with men who supported a 'Federal Parliament' in Ireland. This system of government was too much of a compromise for Young Ireland.

A Federal government would be tied much more closely to London than a Repeal government would, and for Duffy, Dillon and Davis this was out of the question. When Dan announced a new preference for Federalism, Young Ireland was incensed. Gavan Duffy wrote a lengthy article in *The Nation* insisting that Repeal was the only answer to Ireland's problems. The split in the National Association of Ireland was now clear and Dan made an urgent trip to Dublin to address the matter.

While hastening through the country, the Liberator was reassured that his popularity was still intact. Dinners, public addresses and torchlit processions marked his progress from Kerry to the capital. Once in Dublin, he reassured the Young Ireland leaders that Repeal was his ultimate goal; Federalism was something he had merely considered. Still, a wound had been opened, and it would not quickly heal.

In the meantime, Peel attempted to gain Irish support of his own by bringing in some reforms. After the proposal of one of these reforms, the colleges bill, the rift between Dan and the men of Young Ireland re-emerged. Peel's bill would allow new third-level colleges to be open to both Catholics and Protestants. As part of the proposal, the new colleges would not teach religion of any kind. Young Ireland, whose leaders were both Catholic and Protestant, supported the idea. Dan, on the other hand, was furious at such a proposal. He believed secular teaching had no place in a country so full of Catholics. To him, the whole idea was 'Godless'.

A bitter debate on the issue soon followed at a National Association of Ireland meeting at Conciliation Hall on 26 May 1845. Dan accused Thomas Davis and *The Nation* of being anti-Catholic. As for Young Ireland, Dan assured all in the hall that there was no such party.

'I shall stand by Old Ireland. And I have some slight notion that Old Ireland will stand by me.'

Davis first attempted to win back favour by explaining his position, and emphasising his strong affection for Dan. But the young writer and poet had been shaken by Dan's attack and he paused for a moment, before collapsing in tears.

There was a silence.

Dan then rushed to Davis' side, thanked him for the kind words, embraced him and cried out, 'Davis, I love you.'

But no amount of public affection and forgiveness could mend the split in the National Association of Ireland.

Peel, by announcing his reforms for Ireland, had unwittingly destroyed Dan's agitation by sowing such discord among its members.

But something more troubling than the struggle for simple Repeal had already begun to cast a shadow over the country. Black clouds edged in over Ireland in the middle of that summer of 1845. It rained and rained. It rained more in two weeks in July than it had for the previous four months. But even the torrents which fell could not keep down a stench that began to rise from the earth. The smell of death that began to waft from fields would be the first sign of a calamity far greater than either Dan or Peel could ever imagine.

FAMINE, SLAVERY AND YOUNG IRELAND: 1845–6

In September 1845 Dan was back by the roaring Atlantic at Derrynane. It proved a fateful month in Irish history. A great natural disaster struck the land. It came in the form of a fungal disease called *phytophthora infestans*, commonly known as potato blight. The disease, which originated on the east coast of America, had first appeared in Europe in 1843. Now, two years later, it had made its way back across

the Continent, after destroying potato harvests in Germany, Switzerland, Scandinavia and France.

The first reports of the disease in Ireland caused little alarm. There had been a large area sown that year and the potato 'earlies' of August had been of excellent quality. In any case, Ireland had experienced many potato shortages before, mainly due to seasons of excess rain or, sometimes, drought. But the disease that appeared now was different, and it would change the country dramatically, and forever.

In mid-September, however, it was still some weeks before the true effect of the disease would be known. Dan suddenly got word that Thomas Davis had died in Dublin from scarlet fever. He had been only thirty. Although the men differed greatly – in age, in religion and in their ideals – there was still a mutual bond through their work for Ireland.

'My mind is bewildered and my heart afflicted,' Dan wrote to *The Freeman's Journal.* 'The loss of my beloved friend, my noble-minded friend, is a source of the deepest sorrow to my mind. What a blow – what a cruel blow to the cause of Irish nationality!'

Davis had been the chief writer of *The Nation,* with a liking for both ultra-nationalist poetry and dangerous prose. After his death, he was succeeded by John Mitchel, who proved to be even more controversial. In November Mitchel wrote an article describing how the brand-new railway lines being constructed across the country could be dismantled if British troops were making their way through the countryside by train.

Given that *The Nation* and Young Ireland were still part of the National Association of Ireland, Dan was furious with such bloodthirsty language. At the next meeting at Conciliation Hall, he condemned the article outright. He also refused to show any sympathy towards Charles Gavan Duffy, the editor of *The Nation,* when he was put on trial for the matter afterwards.

Another issue dividing Dan and the Young Irelanders was slavery. While Dan was always in favour of human rights, come what may, both Gavan Duffy and Mitchel were critical of Dan showing such support for a 'foreign' cause. Indeed, when Mitchel himself landed on the shores of America some years later, his wish was to have a 'slave plantation, well stocked with slaves'.

Repeal associations had been set up in places like New Orleans and Baltimore to help the struggle in Ireland. They shut down overnight, however, once Dan became involved in the business of anti-slavery. Along with Catholic Emancipation, Dan never wavered on his thoughts on slavery. He cared not one jot what the outcome.

In late 1845 he was giving a talk at Conciliation Hall on, among other things, a Repeal meeting he had attended in Tipperary. It so happened that into the hall stepped Frederick Douglass, a man who had himself just escaped from slavery in the United States. Douglass had earlier seen Dan cross Sackville Street Bridge on his way to Conciliation Hall. The American visitor had been amused to see a group of little boys dressed in rags shouting 'There goes Dan! There goes Dan!' The dark-cloaked Liberator had gazed down upon the urchins with a look brimming with fondness and delight. He had, said Douglass, 'the kindly air of a loving parent returning to his gleeful children ... a more beautiful and touching picture it has seldom been my good fortune to witness'.

In the packed Conciliation Hall, Douglass stood among the congregation when Dan changed the subject from Repeal to American slavery. The Liberator referred to an article in a journal, the *Brownson Review,* in which he had attacked the system.

'I am not ashamed of that attack,' said Dan, from the top of the hall. 'I am the advocate of civil and religious liberty all over the globe. Wherever tyranny exists, I am the foe of the tyrant. Wherever oppression shows itself, I am the foe of the oppressor. Wherever slavery shows its head, I am the enemy of the system, or the institution. Call it what name you will.'

Ever since Emancipation had been won, Dan had been particularly harsh on American slave owners and their government, and that country's idea of what freedom meant. He denounced the tyrannical system in America, and the cruelties of slave owners, wherever he went. A visiting American supporter of Repeal had once stretched out his hand to shake Dan's. The Liberator asked if the gentleman was a slave owner. 'Certainly, sir,' came the reply. 'Then I have no hand for you,' spat Dan.

Dan had once addressed these American 'freemen' directly: 'Dare not stand up boasting of your freedom and your privileges, while you continue to treat men, redeemed by the same blood, as the mere creatures of your will. For while you do so, there is a blot on your coat of arms which all the waters of the Atlantic cannot wash away.'

No one was safe from his ire. Even the first American President, George Washington, already in his grave, had incurred his wrath at a meeting in

Birmingham in 1838. Washington had owned slaves, and had freed them only before his death in 1799. At the same meeting in Birmingham, Dan had so insulted the American Ambassador to Britain, Andrew Stevenson, that the Liberator was challenged to a duel. Dan accused Stevenson of being a slave 'breeder' – seen as a far worse crime than being a slave owner. When Stevenson asked Dan to clarify his comments, he did so in a letter to the local *Morning Chronicle*. Far from apologise, or take back his words, he implied in the letter that Stevenson was no more than 'a disgrace to human nature'. Having worked up Stevenson's anger, Dan, predictably, turned down the pistol fight on moral grounds. At the same time, John Quincy Adams, another former US President, condemned both Stevenson and his appointed second, General James Hamilton, for their involvement in this controversy.

No amount of controversy or loss of support would ever alter Dan's opinions on the plague of slavery in America. At a public meeting in Cork in 1843, after his position on the subject had been challenged from many quarters, he held firm: 'Yes, I will say, shame upon every man in America, who is not an anti-slavery man; shame and disgrace upon him! I don't care for the consequences. I will not restrain my honest indignation of feeling. I pronounce every man a faithless miscreant who does not take a part for the abolition of slavery.'

Dan's booming voice had won over the Corn Exchange that night; the place was deafened with resounding cheering.

Two years later, to the awe of Frederick Douglass and the delight of the crowd at that meeting in Conciliation Hall, he was beating the same drum for human rights. When Douglass took to the roads and byways on a tour of Ireland shortly afterwards, he began to under-stand where Dan's sympathy for human suffering had come from.

'Ireland is threatened with a thing that is read of in history and in distant countries,' read *The Spectator* newspaper on 25 October 1845. 'But scarcely in our own land and time – a famine.' Whole fields of potatoes had, by that stage, rotted in the ground. Many families' sole food provisions for the year had been destroyed.

The greatest crisis in Irish life began just at the moment the sun began to set on Dan's. Still, even with his health and spirits declining, he mustered all the effort he could to save the Irish people. He was chief of a committee at the Mansion House in Dublin to investigate the reasons for the potato failure. With the help of fellow members, including both Whigs and Repealers, he led a small delegation to the Lord Lieutenant's lodge in the Phoenix Park. The committee sought an immediate stop to all exports of corn and other food provisions. Ports were to be opened for the cheap and unrestricted import of food. Dan's committee also sought restrictions on the use of grain for distilling alcohol, and the establishment of food depots throughout the country to provide for the starving poor. Public works were also proposed as a way to provide jobs for the people.

The Lord Lieutenant, Heytesbury, dismissed the suggestions. The Government chose to ignore the committee, and instead favoured the findings of three 'scientists' sent on a research mission to Ireland. Their findings brought word of the catastrophe back to London, but did little else. This trio of Playfair, Lindley and Kane came up with several contradictory remedies for the dying spud, all of which were useless. They were quickly dismissed by *The Freeman's Journal* as men who knew 'nothing whatever about the cause of, or remedies for, the disease'. Even *The Times* of London, no friend to Ireland and bulwark of the Establishment, labelled the scientists' effort as 'vain ... unsatisfactory and idle in its suggestions'.

Dan was harsher still. Indeed, at the next Repeal meeting he was furious: 'One single peck of oats, one bushel of wheat, aye – one boiled potato – would be better than all their reports!'

In the cold light of day, after all reports had been submitted, almost half of the potato crop for 1845 had failed. This finally convinced Robert Peel that the Corn Laws must be abolished. As catastrophe was also sweeping through the industrial north of England, he made a concerted effort to achieve his goal and allow cheap food to be sold in the marketplace. The Corn Laws sought to protect the wealthier farmers by keeping prices high, while not flooding the market with cheaper foods. As this was a key Tory policy, Peel was inviting the wrath of his own party. Inevitably, a division within the Cabinet occurred, and Peel handed in his resignation on 6 December.

Dan hoped that a new administration led by the Whig Lord John Russell would bring dramatic reforms, but those hopes were short-lived. After Russell failed to form a government, Peel was recalled as Prime Minister at Christmas. Although Dan loathed Peel, the Prime Minister did make some efforts to prevent starvation, like buying in excessively cheap 'Indian corn' for sale at an equally low price. Peel also organised the building of roads on the 'board of works' to provide some kind of employment, however laborious that work turned out to be. *The Freeman's Journal* even praised Peel in 1847 when it said: 'No man died of famine during his administration, and it is a boast of which he might well be proud.'

But if Peel showed a certain small generosity on one hand, he was waving a harsh stick in the other. He had a brutal new coercion bill drawn up in early 1846 to deal with fresh outbreaks of crime, which had naturally arisen at a time of such hardship. Among other harsh measures, the new bill proposed a 14-year sentence of transportation to any man found outdoors in troubled spots between sunset and sunrise.

Challenging this bill, known as the 'Protection of Life bill', would be Dan's final great victory in Parliament. His appearances at the House of Commons had become increasingly rare. He was growing old and infirm, but the new bill demanded he make for London to challenge the Government. While cooped up at his hotel on Jermyn Street, Dan wrote to his son Maurice to tell him he must attempt to get 'a ton or two of maize' from Cork in order to feed the poor of Derrynane. It was the early days of the Famine, but food was already running out. Such was the scarcity of food in Kerry that even Dan's beloved beagles were going to go short: 'The dogs must not be fed to the detriment of the poor and we must, at all events, secure our own tenants from destitution.'

With these thoughts of impoverished Ireland, Dan entered the House of Commons on 3 April 1846. His argument to defeat the coercion bill was not a battle cry, for he could barely be heard. His voice, once loud and full of authority, had now broken to a whisper. He had to sit rather than stand, as his once tall and sturdy body was now bent and weak. Still, his address lasted for over two hours, was transcribed for the reporters in the overhead gallery, and promptly appeared in the next day's newspapers. Having read the reports, even Dan's old foe Benjamin Disraeli accepted it was one of the Liberator's better arguments. If his body was frail, his mind was still sharp.

Over many weeks Dan battled the coercion bill tooth and nail, and on 26 June it was at last defeated by a curious combination of Whig MPs, Dan's supporters and Tory protectionists. The Whigs had seen their chance to overthrow the Government by rejecting the new bill, while the protectionists were bitterly opposed to the repeal of the Corn Laws. All three factions wanted Peel out of Downing Street, and by their combination of 'no' votes on coercion, he fell from Government for the last time.

And so, Dan was now on the side of the new Government, finally led by Lord Russell. By supporting Russell, he was hoping to win extensive measures that would combat the worsening crisis in Ireland.

'I am proud,' he said in early June, 'to serve under such a leader as Lord John Russell.'

Gone, for the time being at least, were the dreams of a Parliament on College Green. The Irish people now needed the Government to act, to give them some relief, to save them from starvation. Relief measures already in place, such as the dreaded workhouse system, were wretched in the extreme, with the workhouses designed to appeal to no one except the weakest and most destitute. This was not the time, Dan felt, for arguing the case for Repeal.

'Something must be done by the Government for the benefit of the Irish people during the present session,' he concluded.

But back in Dublin, the Young Irelanders in the National Association of Ireland saw things differently. They were tired of Dan's apparent acquiescence to the Government. In *The Nation* they declared openly that his leadership made it 'certain as fate that this generation would accomplish nothing'. When one young firebrand, Thomas Francis Meagher, had risen at an earlier Repeal meeting on 15 June, he spoke of the late Thomas Davis. Davis had been, said Meagher, 'our leader and our prophet'. Dan had missed this meeting, as he had been in London working to bring down Peel's Government. But Tom Steele had attended. By questioning Dan's leadership, Meagher had provoked the ire of 'Honest Tom'. After Steele exchanged heated words with Meagher, he let Dan know about the latest provocation from Young Ireland. Dan vowed to return from London and 'put down this mischievous knot'.

When he was back in Dublin, Dan decided to attack – with peaceful resolutions. At a Repeal meeting on 13 July 1846, he urged every member of the Association to declare his loyalty to peaceful measures at all costs. Repeal was to be reached through moral force, and moral force alone. John Mitchel then stood and attacked these peaceful resolutions. He spoke of the rebels of 1798, which included his father. Those men, he declared, 'thought liberty worth some blood-letting'.

This was Dan's cue: 'Their struggle was of blood and defeated in blood. The means they adopted weakened Ireland and enabled England to carry the Union!'

Dan knew more than any that now was not the time for talk of 'blood-letting'. Not with Ireland, and her would-be troops, on the brink of starvation. He would never be convinced by the ideas of Young Ireland. He insisted at the meeting that the principle of non-violence be accepted by all. 'I drew up this resolution,' he admitted there and then, 'to draw a marked line between Young Ireland and Old Ireland.'

In the end, everyone sided with Dan and voted in favour of the peaceful resolutions – all except Thomas Francis Meagher. Just two weeks later, he voiced his dissent again, along with Mitchel and William Smith O'Brien (who had now sided with Young Ireland). Dan was in London, but in his place was his son John. Mitchel insisted that the division was not on the question of peace or violence; rather, it arose from Dan's close alliance with the Whig Government. Meagher then stood and made an address. His words would be the last act of Young Ireland as part of the National Association of Ireland. He defended the use of violence in the pursuit of freedom: 'Be it for the defence, or be it for the assertion of a nation's liberty, I look upon the sword as a sacred weapon.'

John O'Connell intervened and insisted that the use of such language was in breach of the resolutions laid down by Dan. Smith O'Brien protested that Meagher should be allowed to share his opinion. When Meagher attempted to resume his speech he was ruled 'out of order' once more. At this, Smith O'Brien got up and walked out of the meeting. He was followed by Meagher, Mitchel, Charles Gavan Duffy and a small number of the audience. The split with Young Ireland had come at last, and was final. There, the Repeal movement died on its knees. The whole agitation was now in tatters.

In any case, for the people of Ireland the only real worry and concern was that of survival. That summer of 1846, the potato blight returned, and with it the destruction of the entire crop. The national calamity of the Great Famine was upon the Irish people. Along with Frederick Douglass, the great temperance priest Fr Mathew had begun to recognise the true extent of the ravages of the disaster. On returning to Cork from Dublin in early August he came across a terrible sight: 'I beheld with sorrow one wide waste of putrefying vegetation. In many places the wretched people were seated on the fences of their decaying gardens, wringing their hands, and wailing bitterly the destruction that had left them foodless.'

Similar tales appeared in the newspapers. Now the potato failure was widespread. Up to four million people faced the prospect of starvation, as Russell's Whig Government had proved itself utterly ineffective in addressing Ireland's plight. As the full horror became evident, and thousands began to die, Dan went to Derrynane in an attempt to do what he could for his tenants. When winter set in Dan became weary and tired. He had never felt so helpless.

'A NATION, it is starving,' he wrote to the *Dublin Evening Post*, in December 1846. 'If there be any exceptions, they are so few and far between that they are not worth mentioning or being noticed ... What is to be done? What is to be done?'

When 1847 finally came, he would attempt to do something himself, with what little energy and spirits were left within him.

THE FINAL JOURNEY: 1847

While the Great Famine was sapping the life out of the land, oozing death and fever across the entire island, Dan too fell into a lethargy and a weakness from which he would never recover.

On a cold January morning in 1847 he met his old friend, O'Neill Daunt, by the River Liffey in Dublin. Despite Dan's condition, the friends opted to walk the long route back to the Liberator's house on Merrion Square, as the sun had briefly flashed out from behind the clouds. As they walked, Daunt noticed a weakness in Dan, whose mind, too, was dreadfully unsettled. Daunt concluded that it was not only personal ailments that troubled Dan, but also the terrible famine that had fallen on the country. When asked about his health, Dan replied: 'I am well enough, only that I feel the feebleness of age upon me.'

Despite his condition, Dan's doctors reassured him. They recommended he make a trip to the warmer climes on the Continent to restore a sound mind and body. He agreed to undertake the trip, which would end in Rome with a visit to the tombs of the apostles and a blessing from Pope Pius IX. First, he would make for London in a final attempt to persuade the Government to take drastic measures to relieve the destitute and dying. And so, on 28 January 1847, Dan stepped off Irish soil and departed for the port of Liverpool. He would not see his beloved Ireland again.

In London, in the company of his valet Duggan and son Daniel, Dan checked into the British Hotel on Jermyn Street. It was only a short jaunt to the House of Commons. It was from Westminster Dan had hoped to

202

procure £30 million for famine relief. Alas, even before he made a final appearance in the House of Commons, he knew hope of such assistance was doomed:

Any prospect of relief from Parliament is, in my judgement, daily diminishing,' he wrote to Thomas Ray on 6 February. 'There is, to be sure, a great deal of sympathy and good feeling both in and out of the House ... but there are also many obstacles, and an unwillingness to place upon the British people the burdens absolutely necessary to give efficient relief to Irish misery.

Two days later, Dan addressed Parliament for the last time. The voice that had once boomed across its chambers, toppled governments, denounced slavery and secured reforms for Ireland was no more. He cast a forlorn figure, drooped and downcast. He spoke in whispers, audible only to those closest to him. And yet, it was reported by one newspaper that the silence throughout his speech was interrupted with many utterances of 'Hear, hear'. It was a show of respect given to a prize fighter in his hour of need.

With what little strength he could summon, and with hands outstretched, Dan appealed to the Government for one 'great act of national generosity'. He told the House that if the Government did not act now, one quarter of Ireland's people would soon perish.

'Ireland is in your hands,' he said in conclusion. 'She is in your power. If you do not save her, she cannot save herself.'

With these last words, he received cheers from both sides of the House. So ended Dan's parliamentary career. Lord Russell's Government would ignore his plea.

Dan's steady deterioration continued, and he longed to go home, to spend his final days at Derrynane. Terrible weather prevented him from travelling, however, and the trip to Rome was confirmed when his private chaplain, Fr John Miley, joined him in London. After engaging in some final correspondence for the cause of Ireland, Dan was confined to his bed at the British Hotel. 'Prayer is his only occupation,' Fr Miley wrote on 22 February. He was now, said his loyal priest, 'perfectly prepared for death, and had rather not be diverted from the thought of it'.

Dan mustered enough strength on 1 March to arise from his slumber and write to FitzPatrick in a request to settle his financial affairs. The Liberator knew he would not return home. After all the necessary paperwork had been done, FitzPatrick made haste for England to wish his friend and chief a last goodbye. Dan had by now headed south, and away from London, with a travelling party of Fr Miley, his sons John and Daniel, and his valet Duggan. He had already reached the small seaside town of Hastings when FitzPatrick caught up.

Here, at the Marine Hotel, Dan received a sudden spurt of good spirits. The sun had been shining and the sight of the gorgeous blue waters of the English Channel had truly invigorated him. He even suggested he could live on to a ripe old age: 'My family had the knack of living long. Several of them reached ninety and some even a hundred years of age.'

From Hastings, he made his way to Folkestone, a four-hour, 25-mile trip. The old road lay between the sea cliffs to the right and a burst of high hill and woodland to the left. The scenery reminded Dan of his dear

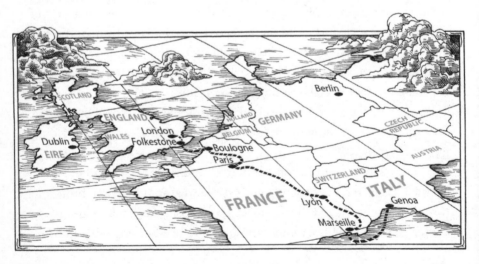

Derrynane, and pleasure shone in his blue eyes. It was Saturday 20 March when his horse-drawn carriage reached Folkestone.

By now the Liberator had been joined by his son-in-law Christopher Fitzsimon, who had become as close to him as any of his offspring. Before Dan departed the coast of England, on the *Prince Ernest* steamboat, he bade his son John, Fitzsimon and FitzPatrick farewell. There, by the Kentish shore, Dan told an emotional FitzPatrick that he had been 'the best of *all* his friends'.

After a safe and peaceful passage to northern France, Dan was soon in the company of his old pal John Gully. The former MP and boxer was relaxing at the Hotel de Bains, in the port of Boulogne. It was obvious to all that Dan was delighted to meet again the man who had once fought sixty-four brutal rounds in just one bout.

Dan then left the last of his old friends behind, as his carriage moved on for Paris by way of the towns of Amiens, Pontoise and Saint-Denis. On arrival in the capital, he took to his bed in the Hotel Windsor as his ailments resurfaced. Yet all the great and good of the city arrived to pay their respects. Archbishop Affre of Paris called at Dan's quarters, along with a delegation of notable French Catholics.

'We are come,' said the bishop, 'to tender you the respectful homage we owe to the man of the age, who has done most for the dignity and liberty of mankind, and especially for the political instruction of Catholic nations ... You are not only the man of one nation, you are the man of all Christendom. Your glory is not only Irish, it is Catholic ... The wishes of Catholic France, of truly liberal France, will accompany you in your pilgrimage to Rome.'

'Gentlemen,' replied Dan, 'it is impossible for me to say what I feel. Know simply that I regard this demonstration as one of the most significant events of my life.'

After a three-day respite, it was time for the party to head off again, now south for Lyon. On the way the sky blackened and snow began to fall. It seemed never to let up.

'How deplorable,' wrote Fr Miley to FitzPatrick on 8 April. 'We are still remorselessly pursued by winter – literally downright wintry weather.'

Dan's strength and appetite were worsening daily. 'The failing of his appetite alarms me greatly,' wrote Miley. 'It will disable him of bearing the fatigue of what yet remains of our journey to Lyon.'

But Dan was made of sterner stuff, and after a twelve-day journey from Paris he arrived in Lyon in one piece. Still, with his face grown thin and a deep sadness in his expression, it was clear the journey had taken its toll.

'I am but the shadow of what I was, and I can scarcely recognise myself,' he told a visiting physician, Dr Bonnet. Dan could barely move his arms, and his right trembled continuously. His left hand and foot were cold and could not be warmed. His step was slow and wavering. Dr Bonnet concluded that his weakness was due to slow congestion of the brain. Dan spent many days lying on his sofa at the Hotel of the Universe. Masses were said in all of Lyon's churches for his recovery.

After eleven days in the city, Dan recovered just enough strength to depart, and strike for Marseilles. At the dock on the River Rhône, a reporter from the *Gazette de Lyon* watched as he stepped aboard a southbound steamboat, and later wrote: 'How, said we to ourselves, is this, indeed, the man who has filled the world with the thunder of his name, and made England tremble to her centre? We see Ireland weakened, and bent down, and lingering, in the person of her illustrious champion. God protect O'Connell and Ireland.'

Dan, Fr Miley, Duggan and Daniel were joined by another of Lyon's medical men, Dr Lacour. They descended the Rhône at ease, through Valence, Avignon and Arles, before reaching Marseilles. As they coasted to the Mediterranean, the weather improved, and so too did Dan's health. He joined in conversation with more strength and interest. Hopes rose that he would make it to Rome. On Wednesday 5 May, he boarded the *Lombardo*.

France was soon a memory as, just a day later, the spires of the great port of Genoa in Italy were in sight. The weather was magnificent, and

for the first two days of his stay at the Hotel Feder there was a further improvement in Dan's health. On the third day, however, the Liberator complained of a bad pain in his head, no doubt from congestion of the brain. His pulse quickened, his speech accelerated and his movements became more energetic. At night he was unable to sleep, such was the anxiety he felt at death's approach.

Fr Miley was desperate to make for Rome, but Dan was depressed and refused to move. Miley despaired, for the weather was good and a boat passage was surely easy: 'From where we are the journey to Rome is like gliding down a sunny stream. Yet go he says he cannot. The will of God be done! I am heartbroken at this issue.'

It became tragically clear that the decision to stay was the last right one made by the great and noble Dan. The end was near. On the night of 13 May he was struck with an intense delirium. He imagined himself playing pranks with his grand-children at Derrynane. In the Genoa night, he saw Robert Peel there in front of him in the House of Commons.

From his deathbed, Dan shouted: 'I have got the Repeal! Hurrah! I have got it safely locked in a box!'

He took the hand of his valet, Duggan, and told him: 'You are the only person I can depend on ... Do not let them bury me until after I am dead.'

The clock ticked; the minutes and hours dragged on. The prayers of Fr Miley were futile. Finally, at 2 a.m. on Saturday 15 May 1847, the priest knew Dan's time had come. It was the hour for the Liberator to receive the last sacraments. Father Miley sent for the viaticum and the holy oil. The Cardinal Archbishop of Genoa arrived along with several of his clergy. Dan's hands were clasped in prayer and he was in perfect possession of his mind while he received the last rites. As day broke and morning turned into afternoon, he could be heard murmuring in worship: 'Jesus ... Jesus ...'

At six o'clock Dan pulled Miley towards him and whispered, 'My dear friend, I am dying.' Throughout the evening a low Italian lilt could be heard in prayer all about the Hotel Feder. At one stage the bedframe shook as the great Dan made one last struggle. At 9.37 p.m., all movement ceased. The flame that had burned for seventy-one years had been extinguished. The Liberator was dead.

Dan never reached Rome – but his heart did. At a funeral Mass in the Italian capital, it was said that Dan had requested his heart to be entombed in the holy city. And so it was, at the Church of Sant'Agata dei Goti.

Dan's body reached Ireland in August, on board the steamboat *Duchess of Kent*. As it sailed up the River Liffey, it was met by an outbound emigrant ship, the *Birmingham*, full of passengers fleeing the Famine. All aboard began to keen for their dead chief. While many Irish people died with him in 1847, many more survived, and left behind Old Ireland forever.

In his lifelong struggle for Repeal, his commitment to the abolition of slavery, and his constant battle on behalf of the downtrodden of his own land, Dan had taught that generation never to rest in the pursuit of national liberty or the fight for human rights. By breaking down the door to power and winning Catholics their Emancipation, the Liberator had

208

taught them that they were as good as the next person, wherever they were, or wherever they went.

He taught the Catholics of Ireland how to straighten their backs, and how to hold their heads up high.

In devoting his life to Ireland and her people – hit or miss, win or lose – Daniel O'Connell ensured his name would live forever in our history.

GLOSSARY

1798 Rebellion: a rebellion led by the United Irishmen against British rule in Ireland, which lasted from May to September 1798

abolitionist: person in favour of banning slavery

Act: a law

aggregate meeting: a meeting of a large body (in this case, Catholics)

agrarian: relating to the land

American War of Independence: armed conflict between Britain and its American colonies, resulting in American independence

annus horribilis: a year of disaster and/or misfortune

Anti-Corn Law League: movement in Britain aimed at abolishing the Corn Laws

assize: court held periodically in towns for serious offences

Attorney General: the head of a country's legal department

the Bar: the legal profession

be called to the Bar: be qualified to speak for another in a court of law

bench: the seat of a judge in court

bill: the formal proposal for a new law. If successful, a bill becomes an Act

bough: green plant carried as an emblem of peace

Cabinet: senior ministers of the Government

cant: insincere talk

canvass: to campaign for votes

Catholic Emancipation: reducing and removing restrictions on Roman Catholics, such as the ability to sit in Parliament

Cato: Roman statesman famous for his oratory, determination and stubbornness

cavalry: soldiers on horseback

Chief Secretary: the government minister for Ireland, responsible for the country's rule. Lower in rank to the Lord Lieutenant, the Chief Secretary had, nevertheless, more direct power

Classics: the study of the literature, philosophy and history of ancient Greece and Rome

constitution: the principles by which a state is governed

Convention Act of 1793: an Act declaring any assembly that claimed to represent the people, other than the Government, illegal

Corn Laws: laws protecting high prices on bread. Good for landowners, but not for the poor who relied on the food to survive

coronation: the act or ceremony of crowning a new King or Queen

cottier: farm labourer paid in small land holding and cabin, rather than cash

Deism: belief that God exists in nature, and is not a supernatural being

demesne: land belonging to and adjoining a manor house; estate

Dominican: Roman Catholic religious order founded in the thirteenth century to preach the Gospel

duel: formal, arranged combat fought to settle a point of honour

epicure: a person devoted to the pleasures of life, especially food

extremism: supporting extreme measures and views

Federal Parliament: a proposal for Parliament in Ireland that would deal with local affairs only, leaving final authority with Westminster in London

fife: high-pitched flute

foppery: the clothing of a vain man

French Revolution: period of social and political upheaval from 1789 until 1799 that overthrew the reigning monarchy and established a republic

frieze coat: common heavy-duty coat of the nineteenth century

garrison: a military camp/base

gibbet: a gallows with a projecting arm at the top, from which the bodies of criminals were formerly hung in chains, and left suspended after execution

governess: a woman who teaches and trains children in a private household

GR: short for *Georgius Rex*, the Latin for King George, and on p. 117 used within the stamp of the reigning monarch

Henry Grattan (1746–1820): Irish Protestant politician and member of the Irish House of Commons; campaigner for the legal independence of that Parliament in the late eighteenth century (secured in 1782)

Home Office: department responsible for domestic matters, such as elections and law and order

Home Secretary: responsible for affairs of law and order within the 'home' islands of the United Kingdom of Great Britain and Ireland

jejune: dull and childish

to keen: a loud wailing or lament for the dead

laurel: leaf and branch traditionally taken from the bay tree

Legion: army unit

libel: a method of insult expressed in print

liberal: politics not opposed to new ideas

Lord Lieutenant: the British Monarch's official representative in Ireland from 1801 to 1922

magistrate: an officer of the law

martial law: harsh military law imposed when law and order breaks down

mutineer: one who revolts against the navy or military

Napoleon Bonaparte (1769–1821): French military and political leader who rose to power during the French Revolution

novena: Catholic devotion of nine days' prayer and/or service

Oliver Cromwell (1599–1658): English military man who led the conquest of Ireland in a violent campaign from 1649 to 1653

opposition: the party(s) not in power

Orange Order: society founded in 1795 to defend Irish Protestants and favouring the Union of Great Britain and Ireland

Orangemen: members of the Orange Order

Ossianic: of the epic poetry of the Irish bard Ossian, or Oisín, dealing with the Fenian cycle

packet ship: a regular, scheduled sea service carrying passengers and freight

papist: slang term for a Roman Catholic

parliamentary reform: improving or modernising Parliament

Patriot Party: eighteenth-century Irish party that supported a Whig government and Irish identity, but rejected full independence

patronage: power given to people as a reward for their support

peer: a member of any of the five degrees of the nobility (duke, marquis, earl, viscount and baron)

Penal Laws: harsh measures designed to deny Catholics of all rights, and subject them to the complete rule of the Protestant British Establishment

perjurer: a person who lies in court after taking the oath

pike: a weapon with a heavy spear on the end of a long shaft

proclamation: an official announcement

radical: person who supports complete political and/or social change

rector: Protestant clergyman

Reform: to change or modernise the state of a country's governance

Robert Emmet (1778–1803): Irish nationalist and republican, orator and rebel leader

royal assent: the final stage of the legislative process, when the King (or Queen) signs off an Act to become law

rushlight: a candle formed by dipping the rush plant in fat or grease

second: a duellist's assistant

sectarian: concerning different sections of society, in this case Protestants and Catholics

secular: not relating to religion or a religious body

servitude: the state of being a slave

Solicitor General: a chief law officer who defends the rights of the state

squireen: Irish slang for a minor gentleman

temperance: abstaining from consuming alcohol

tithes: money paid to the Protestant Church of Ireland for its upkeep

Tory: major British political party favouring Royal authority and the defeat of reform in Parliament

transportation: banishment of a prisoner to a penal colony

traverser: someone who crosses a line, like a criminal

treason: a violation of allegiance to the state

typhus: fatal fever caused by filth and overcrowding

ultra-Protestant: religious extremist, with prejudices against other religions, especially Catholicism

untie the Gordian knot: to solve a problem quickly and boldly

veto: the veto was the right of the Government to deny a bishop's appointment, if they had 'any proper objection'. In return, the Government would provide state payment to the clergy

viaticum: communion given to a dying person

Whig: major British political party that wanted to decrease Royal power and increase the power of Parliament

Yeomanry: volunteer unit of the British army used to quell riots and civil disturbances

BIBLIOGRAPHY

Beckett, J. C., *The Making of Modern Ireland, 1603–1923* (London, Faber and Faber, 1966)

Cusack, Mary F., *Life of Daniel O'Connell, the Liberator* (New York, D. & J. Sadlier, 1885)

Daunt, William J. O'Neill, *Life and Times of Daniel O'Connell* (Dublin, Mullany, 1867)

Daunt, William J. O'Neill, *Personal Recollections of the Late Daniel O'Connell, M.P.* (London, Clapman and Hall, 1848)

Donnelly, James S., *Captain Rock: The Irish Agrarian Rebellion of 1821–1824* (Cork, The Collins Press, 2009)

Elliot, Marianne, *Wolfe Tone: Prophet of Irish Independence* (Yale University Press, 1989)

Fagan, William, *The Life and Times of Daniel O'Connell* (Cork, J. O'Brien, 1847–8)

Fenton, Laurence, *Frederick Douglass in Ireland: The 'Black O'Connell'* (Cork, The Collins Press, 2014)

FitzPatrick, William J., *Correspondence of Daniel O'Connell, the Liberator* (London, J. Murray, 1888)

Foster, R. F., *Modern Ireland 1600–1972* (London, Penguin, 1988)

Geoghegan, Patrick M., *King Dan: The Rise of Daniel O'Connell, 1775–1829* (Dublin, Gill & Macmillan, 2008)

Geoghegan, Patrick M., *Liberator: The Life and Death of Daniel O'Connell 1830–1847* (Dublin, Gill & Macmillan, 2010)

Gray, Peter, *The Irish Famine* (London, Thames & Hudson, 1995)

Gwynn, Denis, *Daniel O'Connell: The Irish Liberator* (London, Hutchinson & Co., 1929)

Houston, Arthur, *Daniel O'Connell: His Early Life and Journal, 1795 to 1802* (London, Sir I. Pitman, 1906)

Kee, Robert, *The Green Flag: Volume One, The Most Distressful Country* (Harmondsworth, Penguin, 1989)

MacDonagh, Michael, *The Life of Daniel O'Connell* (London/New York, Cassell, 1903)

MacDonagh, Oliver, *The Hereditary Bondsman* (London, Weidenfeld and Nicholson, 1988)

MacDonagh, Oliver, *The Emancipist: Daniel O'Connell 1830–47* (London, Weidenfeld and Nicholson, 1989)

O'Connell, Maurice R., *The Correspondence of Daniel O'Connell* (8 volumes) (Dublin, Irish University Press, 1972–7)

O'Ferrall, Fergus, *Daniel O'Connell* (Dublin, Gill & Macmillan, 1981)

O'Flanagan, J. R., *The Munster Circuit: Tales, Trials and Traditions* (London, Sampson Low, Marston, Searle & Rivington, 1880)

Trench, Charles C., *The Great Dan: A Biography of Daniel O'Connell* (London, J. Cape, 1984)

Vaughan, W. E. (ed.), *A New History of Ireland – Ireland under the Union 1801–70* (Oxford, Clarendon, 1996)

ACKNOWLEDGMENTS

Anyone who works on a book of this nature owes a huge debt to those who came before. This book is no different. Biographers of Daniel O'Connell, both in his own time and modern times, have laid down a huge swathe of material that is invaluable, abundant and often brilliant.

Dan's own colleague, William Joseph O'Neill Daunt, wrote about the great man's life as it happened. With a mammoth two-volume biography and a book of Dan's own recollections, Daunt captured a man who was funny, gregarious, theatrical, offensive, bashful and supremely self-confident. Above all he shows us a man who was serious about the cause of Ireland, and the liberty of her people. The work of Denis Gwynn has also been invaluable in the research for this book, as has that of Michael MacDonagh and Dan's modern biographer, Patrick Geoghegan. Two great books have pride of place on my shelf: the two-volume O'Connell biography written by Oliver MacDonagh in the 1980s. My own small work is in the playground that is the city of these great chunks of Irish history writing.

Special thanks to Eoin O'Driscoll who proofread the text in its entirety. His tremendous knowledge of the subject proved a huge addition to the finished work. Joe Culley, a former subeditor with *The Irish Times*, has been with me as a subeditor on this project. His contribution has been invaluable and brilliant. He is owed the sincerest and humblest thanks. A great and warm thanks also to Sinead Moylan and Josie O'Brien who both read the original draft from start to finish, and contributed in no small way.

Gratitude to Edward O'Carroll for his help on social media, and to Emmet Farrell for his brilliant contribution to the initial submission. Alison Burns, of Burns Design, is due the highest praise and thanks for her work on the design of this book.

Both myself and the book's illustrator – Mateusz Nowakowski – would like to thank our parents, Jackie and Annie Moylan, and Pawel Nowakowski and Marta Nowakowska.

Our friends and family are all owed the fondest of acknowledgements. Gratitude to Patricia, Michael, Sean, Fionuala, Thomas, Colm, Adrian, Janina, Bart, Kasia and Rut. Special thanks also to Dorota, John, Kate, Rita, Suzanne and David.

To anyone who takes the time to read and take something from this book, you too are thanked. Any mistakes or inaccuracies are mine, and mine alone. As with the rest of the book, it has been an honour to write all these words.